MW00380872

5th Grade

Reading + Writing

& Essay

ELA WORKBOOK

BOBBY-TARIQ

© COPYRIGHT 2019 BY BOBBY TARIQ TUTORIAL INC.

All rights reserved.

No part of this publication may be reproduced, distributed, or transmitted in any form or by any means, including photocopying, recording, or other electronic or mechanical methods, without the prior written permission of the publisher, except in the case of brief quotations embodied in critical reviews and certain other noncommercial uses permitted by copyright law.

ISBN   9781090329554

BOBBY TARIQ TUTORIAL INC.
7409 37th Ave
Jackson heights, NY 11372
www.bobbytariq.com

Table of Content

<u>Worksheet 1</u>

<u>Directions</u>: Read the rewritten passage of "The Gift of the Magi" by O. Henry. Then answer questions 1-6.

The Gift of the Magi

(1)   One dollar and eighty-seven cents were all Della had in her pocket, and sixty cents of it was in pennies. These were pennies saved one and two at a time by not leaving a tip for the grocer or the vegetable man or the butcher. Her cheeks were red with the silent embarrassment of being cheap. Three times Della counted the money. It was still one dollar and eighty-seven cents, and the next day would be Christmas.

(2)   There was clearly nothing left to do but sit down on the shabby little couch and cry. So, Della did it. She really needed more money to buy Christmas presents.

(3)   While Della is sad and angry with her situation, take a look at her home. A furnished apartment for $8 per week. It did not exactly look like a beggar's apartment, but it certainly had that slight look of a beggar's apartment.

(4)   In the entranceway was a mailbox into which no letter would go, and a doorbell from which no one ever came to ring. Also, there was a nameplate on the outside of the door bearing the name "Mr. James Dillingham Young."

(5)   Della's husband, James Dillingham Young, or Jim as he was called, had been making $30 per week for his weekly pay from work. Now, when the income was shrunk to $20, the letters of "Dillingham" looked blurred. It was as though the letters were telling the Dillinghams that they should be seriously thinking of moving to a cheaper place. Whenever Mr. James Dillingham Young came home and reached his apartment he was called "Jim" and greatly hugged by Mrs. James Dillingham Young, already introduced to you as Della.

(6)   Della finished crying and attended to her cheeks with the powder rag. She stood by the window and looked out at a grey cat walking a grey fence in a grey backyard. Tomorrow would be Christmas Day, and she had only $1.87 with which to buy Jim a present. She had been saving every penny she could for months with the result of $1.87. Twenty dollars a week doesn't go far. Expenses had been greater than she had thought. They always are. Only $1.87 to buy a present for Jim. This was her Jim. Many happy hours she had spent planning for something nice for him. She was thinking of something fine and rare and sterling--something just a little bit more than what they usually bought, so it would be owned by Jim.

(7)   There was a mirror between the windows of the room. Perhaps you have seen these mirrors in an $8 apartment. A very thin person may, by observing his reflection in a rapid

sequence of long strips of the mirror, obtain a fairly good grasp of his looks. Della, being slender, had mastered the art of looking into this mirror.

(8)   Suddenly she whirled from the window and stood before the glass. Her eyes were shining brilliantly, but her face had lost its color within twenty seconds. Rapidly she pulled down her hair and let it fall to its full length.

(9)   Now, there were two valuable possessions of the James Dillingham Youngs in which they were both proud of. One was Jim's gold watch that had been his father's and his grandfather's. The other was Della's hair. Her hair was both beautiful and valuable. For, during this time hair was worth a lot of money to be made into expensive wigs. Wigmakers were always willing to pay top money for beautiful hair. As far as Della's hair, if the Queen of Sheba had lived in the apartment across from her, the Queen would have valued Della's hair even more than her own jewels. If King Solomon passed by Jim as he pulled out his watch, King Solomon would have admired it.

1. What comparison can be made based on the connection between James Dillingham Youngs and the Queen of Sheba/King Solomon?
    A. The queen and king said they would exchange their jewels for Della's hair and Jim's watch.
    B. The queen and king have jewels that could be sold for the same amount of money as Jim's watch and Della's hair.
    C. The queen and king would envy Della's hair and Jim's watch.
    D. The queen and king lived next door to Della's and Jim's apartment.

2.   Della works hard to buy Jim a good Christmas present. How is her hard work shown in the story?
    A. By saving the money in pennies and counting it so many times
    B. By growing her hair so long so she could sell it
    C. By working at a grocery store for many weeks before Christmas
    D. By asking the grocer, vegetable man and butcher for money.

3. Using the sentence below and what you read about Della's and Jim's financial situation in the story, what does the word **shabby** probably mean?
        There was clearly nothing left to do but sit down on the shabby little couch and cry.
    A. old
    B. ragged
    C. average
    D. unusual

4. How can you tell that the narrator feels sorry for Della's problems with money?
   A. When he explains how Della has beautiful hair that could be sold
   B. When he describes how hard Della is working, but how poor she is
   C. By informing the reader that Della has sixty pennies
   D. By creating a tone of Della not working to support her family

5. In the first paragraph, the narrator describes in detail exactly how much money Della has. Why is this information important at the beginning and then later in the story?
   A. It explains how important it is for Della to be able to buy a good present for her husband.
   B. It describes the exact amount of money Della has in her pocket.
   C. It lets the reader know that she did not fully pay for items from the grocer, vegetable man, and butcher.
   D. It explains how angry Della is for having so little money.

6. What evidence from the text displays the condition of the apartment that Della and Jim live in?
   A. "but it certainly had that slight look of a beggar's apartment."
   B. "In the entranceway was a mailbox into which no letter would go,"
   C. "A furnished apartment for $8 per week."
   D. "It did not exactly look like a beggar's apartment,"

> **Directions**: Read the rewritten passage of "Big Cats In Danger of Extinction." Then answer questions 7-8.

Big Cats in Danger of Extinction

Extinction is Forever

(1)   Some big cats throughout history have become extinct because they were replaced with newer species that were able to live in the environment. The Sabretooth is one example of a large Ice-Age predator that died out because the large prey it needed to eat died. Pumas and jaguars now roam where the mighty Sabretooth once ruled. Natural extinction is part of life on Earth. However, many more cat species are in danger of dying out due to unnatural extinction, which is the killing of an entire species by man for reasons having nothing to do surviving in the wild. These species are not replaced with newer ones, but their death makes mankind look bad for what they have done.

Predation

(2)   Many big cats have been killed because they either compete with humans for the same prey animals or because they occasionally attack human-raised livestock. Some big cats that become too weak to hunt their own natural prey find a farmer's livestock much simpler to kill. Other big cats develop a taste for livestock because it is easy to do. There are times when killing these predators, through moving or killing, appear to be accepted and approved. However, there is a much more dangerous approach to controlling these predators where an entire population or even an entire species is classified as a "pest" and open to execution.

(3)   Extermination is an attempt to kill every last individual of a population or species. There were times when pumas were targeted for extermination in large areas of the American West. Bobcats and jaguars have also been targets of extermination. These days most governments in the world agree that extermination is not a good way to control cats, but sometimes local people ignore laws to protect species from extermination.

Sport Hunting

(4)   The majority of people in North and South American no longer give big game hunters the same respect they once had long ago. The cheetah, which was once abundant in India, was hunted to complete extinction there. The Mughal emperor Akbar killed nearly 1000 cheetahs during his lifetime when the number of cheetahs was already declining. The same happened to the Asian lion.

(5)   Most outdoorsmen no longer seek trophies for their mantles and entrance halls. However, a number of people still consider locating, tricking, and killing large predators to be the very courageous and a satisfying form of enjoying the outdoors. This practice is losing popularity, though.

7. Describe the ways that extinction and extermination support the two main ideas of this text.

_____

_____

_____

_____

_____

_____

_____

_____

8. How does the author support his claim that the animals should be protected and not be killed? Cite 3 pieces of evidence from the text to support your explanation.

_____

_____

_____

_____

_____

_____

_____

_____

Directions: Read the rewritten passage of "Babylonians." Then answer questions 9-11.

Babylonians

What country did they live in?

(1)   The Babylonians lived in what is now modern-day Iraq. They controlled much of the land between the rivers, Tigris and the Euphrates. They were the last of the city states (civilizations based around a single powerful city) to control this area. In the 24th century BC the city of Babylon was founded on the banks of the Euphrates River. In the 18th century BC it became a capital of Babylonian empire.

Walls of Babylon

(2)   Babylon reached its glory in 6th century BC. Constructions like the Ishtar Gate and Etemenanki ziggurat were built, making Babylon the most beautiful city in the ancient world. Ishtar Gate was one of the eight gates of the Babylon city. Dedicated to the goddess Ishtar, the Gate was constructed of blue glazed tiles with alternating rows of dragons and bulls. The roof and doors of the gate were made of cedar. Through the gate ran the Processional Way, which was lined with walls covered in lions on glazed bricks (about 120 of them). Statues of the gods were paraded through the gate and down the Processional Way each year during the New Year's celebration.

What did they eat?

(3)   The Babylonians ate melons, plums, prunes and dates. Barley was their staple crop that they would make flat breads with. The bread would then be eaten with some fruit. For meat they ate pork, poultry, beef, fish and mutton (sheep meat). Onions and garlic were common seasonings for their food. Babylonians didn't drink wine, but instead they drank beer made out of barley.

What did they wear?

(4)   Babylonians wore a garment that would look like a long T-shirt in our day. For the peasants, these garments would have been quite simple but for the wealthy they were decorated with tassels, embroidery, girdles and sashes. Higher ranking people wore longer garments and scarves that indicated their rank by the length of its tassels.

(5)   Hats were also an important fashion accessory. Professionals could be identified by their characteristic headdress. Women wore ribbons, veils or other decorations in their hair.

What did they believe?

(6)   The Babylonians were polytheists which means that they believed that there were many gods that ruled different parts of the universe. They believed that the king god was Marduk, patron of Babylon. Just as Babylon conquered all city states and became the capital of a mighty empire, so, in the legend, its patron Marduk obtained power over other gods by fighting Tiamat, the evil goddess of chaos.

(7)   The Babylonians built each of their gods a primary temple that was considered the home of the god. People would bring sacrifices to the gods, and the priests would try to attend to the needs of the gods through ceremonies and festivals. Each temple had an open temple courtyard and then an inner sanctuary that only the priests could enter. Sometimes special pyramid shaped towers, called ziggurats, were built to be a part of the temples. The top of the tower was a special sanctuary for the god.

(8)   Babylonians believed that after death every soul went to the underworld. The underworld was considered a dark and dismal place. This made death a dreadful event as there was no hope of ever having anything better.

Are some of them famous even today?

(9)   One of Babylon's most famous kings was Hammurabi. He ruled for 43 years. Hammurabi was famous for creating one of the first formal written set of laws. These laws were written on a stone tablet standing over six feet tall. The most famous rule he set is now known as an eye for an eye. This rule said that the punishment for lawbreakers would be the same as the crime they committed. So, if a criminal stabbed a person in the eye, the criminal would be stabbed in the eye too. The laws he made were known as "The Code of Hammurabi". This legal system was spread throughout Asia and Europe. The Code of Hammurabi is also interesting because it was the first set of laws which believed that people were innocent, meaning a person must be proven guilty before they could be punished for their crimes.

What is left of them today?

(10)   The ruins of the city of Babylon still exist although the city has been abandoned for over 2000 years. Many of the inventions of the Babylonians are still important today. They invented metalworking, copper-working, glassmaking, lamp making, textile weaving, flood control, water storage, as well as irrigation. Interestingly, from their number system we get our concept of 60 minutes in an hour and 60 seconds in a minute.

9. Explain how the headings of this passage help the reader identify the main idea of each paragraph. Cite 3 pieces of evidence from the text that supports your explanation.

_____

_____

_____

_____

_____

_____

_____

_____

10. Describe the similarities between Hammurabi's Code and the way that the gods were treated.

_____

_____

_____

_____

_____

_____

_____

_____

11. How was the way the author revealed the meaning of "ziggurat" different from the way the author revealed the meaning of the "underworld?"

_____

_____

_____

_____

_____

_____

_____

_____

Directions: Read the rewritten passage of "The Ransom of Red Chief." Then answer questions 12-13.

The Ransom of Red Chief

(1)   It looked like a good thing, but wait until I tell you. We were down South in Alabama. Bill Driscoll and I were in Alabama when this kidnapping idea struck us. It was, as Bill afterward said it during a moment of stupidity, but we didn't find that out till later.

(2)   There was a town down there as flat as a pancake and it was called Summit. It contained citizens that were like peasants.

(3)   Bill and I had put our money together which came out to six hundred dollars. We needed just two thousand dollars more to pull off a kidnapping in Western Illinois. We talked it over on the front steps of the hotel. It was best to kidnap in a rural setting because newspapers wouldn't be able to send reporters out in plain clothes to stir up talk about such things. We knew that Summit couldn't get after us with anything stronger than a few police officers and maybe some lazy bloodhounds. So, it looked good.

(4)   We selected for our victim the only child of a prominent citizen named Ebenezer Dorset. The father was respectable and cautious about spending. He was a mortgage lender and a strict, upright man. The kid was a boy of ten with freckles and hair the color of the cover of the magazine you buy at the newsstand when you want to catch a train. Bill and I figured that Ebenezer would easily give a ransom of two thousand dollars to a cent. But wait till I tell you.

(5)   About two miles from Summit was a little mountain covered with cedar trees. On the rear side of this mountain was a cave. There we stored our food and supplies.

(6)   One evening after sundown, we drove in a buggy past old Dorset's house. The kid was in the street, throwing rocks at a kitten on the opposite fence.

(7)   "Hey, little boy!" says Bill, "would you like to have a bag of candy and a nice ride?"

(8)   The boy catches Bill neatly in the eye with a piece of brick.

(9)   "That will cost the old man an extra five hundred dollars," says Bill, climbing over the wheel.

(10)   That boy put up a fight like a boxer, but, at last we got him down in the bottom of the buggy and drove away. We took him up to the cave, and I hitched the horse to the cedar tree. After dark I drove the buggy to the little village which was three miles away and walked back to the mountain.

(11)   Bill was treating the scratches and bruises on his face and body. There was a fire burning behind the big rock at the entrance of the cave, and the boy was watching a pot of boiling coffee with two bird tailfeathers stuck in his red hair. He points a stick at me when I come up and yelled at me.

(12)   "Ha! Old Man, do you dare to enter the camp of Red Chief, the terror of the plains?"

(13)   "He's all right now," says Bill, rolling up his trousers and examining some bruises on his shins. "We're playing Indian. We're making Buffalo Bill's show look really cool. I'm Old Hank, the Trapper, Red Chief's captive, and I'm to be scalped at daybreak. That kid can kick hard."

(14)   Yes, sir, that boy seemed to be having the time of his life. The fun of camping out in a cave had made him forget that he was kidnapped. He immediately called me Snake-eye, the Spy, and announced that when his natives returned from the warpath, I was to be killed.

12. Explain how the fourth paragraph, which describes the kidnapped boy's father, contributes to the story.

_____

_____

_____

_____

_____

_____

_____

_____

13. One might say that the theme of this story is that doing the wrong thing may turn out to be even more terrible that one might have thought. Describe how the unexpected events during the kidnapping support that theme.

Be sure to include:
*a description of the theme
*actions by the kidnapped boy
*how the kidnappers respond

_____

_____

_____

_____

_____

_____

_____

_____

_____

_____

_____

_____

_____

CONTINUE

Worksheet 2

The Luck of the Roaring Camp

(1)   There was a loud noise in Roaring Camp. It could not have been a real fight because in 1850 sound of happiness was never heard. The whole camp was collected before a cabin on the outer edge of the clearing. Conversation was carried on in a quiet voice, but the name of a woman was frequently repeated. It was a name familiar enough in the camp, --"Cherokee Sal."

(2)   Perhaps the less said of her the better. She was a coarse and, it is to be feared, a very feared woman. At that time, she was the only woman in Roaring Camp, and was about to give birth. Sal was met disapproving of her masculine associates to bring a baby into this gold prospecting camp. Yet a few of the spectators were, I think, touched by her suffering. Sandy Tipton thought it was "rough on Sal," and in the observation of her condition for a moment he had an idea.

(3)   It will be seen also that the situation was new. Deaths were by no means uncommon in Roaring Camp, but a birth was a new thing. People had been dismissed from the camp effectively, finally and with no possibility of return. This was the first time that anybody had been introduced. That is why there was excitement.

(4)   "You go in there, Stumpy," said a prominent citizen known as "Kentuck," addressing one of the them. "Go in there, and see what you can do. You've had experience in them things."

(5)   Stumpy in other areas had been the assumed head of two families. In fact, it was thought to some extent that Roaring Camp--a city of sanctuary--was obligated to his company. The crowd approved the choice, and Stumpy was wise enough to accept it. The door closed on the makeshift surgeon and midwife, and the people of Roaring Camp sat down outside, smoked their pipes, and awaited the issue.

(6)   The group outside numbered about a hundred men. One or two of these were actual fugitives from justice, some were criminal, and all were reckless. From their appearance, they exhibited no indication of their past lives and character. The greatest troublemaker had an angelic face with a profusion of blonde hair. Oakhurst, a gambler, had a gloomy feeling about him and discreetly smart. The coolest and most courageous man was scarcely over five feet in height with a soft voice and a shy manner. Also having eyes, ears, toes, etc. didn't matter. The strongest man had but three fingers on his right hand, and the best shot had but one eye.

(7)   The same could be said for the physical abilities of the men that were around the cabin. The camp lay in a triangular valley between two hills and a river. The only way out was a steep trail over the summit of a hill that faced the cabin now illuminated by the rising moon. The suffering woman might have seen it from the bunk whereon she lay winding like a silver thread until it was lost in the stars above.

1. Which word below could be used to describe the feelings of the men in the camp towards the pregnant woman in the camp?
    A. Sympathetic
    B. Understanding
    C. Unconcerned
    D. Confused

2. What evidence from the passage supports the idea that Sal was tough enough to belong in the camp?
    A. "It was a name familiar enough in the camp, --"Cherokee Sal."
    B. "Sal was met disapproving of her masculine associates to bring a baby into this gold prospecting camp."
    C. "She was a coarse and, it is to be feared, a very feared woman."
    D. "the name of a woman was frequently repeated."

3. Why did the author include the information in the first paragraph about the noise in the camp?
    A. To describe the contrast in noise of a baby
    B. To create a sense of happiness with the cries of the baby
    C. To explain the scenery of men talking in a camp
    D. To show the anger exhibited by the men in the camp

4. Why might the author have described the strongest man as having only a few fingers on a hand and the man who could shoot the best as having only one eye?
    A. To provide details of the various men who worked in gold mining camps
    B. To display the violence that occurs by gold miners
    C. To reveal the dangers of working in a gold prospecting camp
    D. To show that physical abilities did not always prove talent or strength

5. Based on the descriptions in the passage, how is Stumpy characterized?
    A. As one of the first miners of the camp
    B. As the most successful gold miner
    C. As someone who took the roles of mother and father in his family
    D. As the toughest man in the camp

6. In the passage, what is stated about the noise in the camp?
   A. Common talking is heard among the men in the camp.
   B. Loud noise of fighting is common.
   C. A baby crying cuts the tension in the camp.
   D. A soothing sound of people talking

Directions: Read the rewritten passage of "K-T Event." Then answer questions 7-8.

K-T Event

(1)   Sixty-five million years ago, many different kinds of animals on Earth died out. It is believed that the larger land creatures suffered the most and most animals bigger than a dog disappeared including most dinosaurs!

(2)   Something extraordinary had happened to destroy so much life. Scientists call this event the Cretaceous-Tertiary event (K-T for short). Nobody is sure what the K-T event was, but scientists have some ideas about what might have happened.

Asteroid Explanation
(3)   An asteroid could have hit the Earth. An asteroid is a giant piece of rock moving through space. Very rarely, these asteroids fall on Earth. Some scientists think that an asteroid 10 kilometers wide fell on Earth 65 million years ago. A large asteroid hitting the Earth would cause a huge firestorm and cause a lot of dust to fly into the air. This dust would block out the sun for several months or even for several years.

(4)   With most sunlight blocked by dust, the ground would get colder, and a long winter would come. To make things worse, the large amount of dust in the air would cause acid rain, rain so poisonous that it could harm or even kill plants.

(5)   The combination of the cold, little sun and poisonous rain would kill many plants. Herbivore dinosaurs would not have enough plants left to eat and would starve. Without herbivores to eat, the carnivores would starve too.

(6)   When scientists examine layers of very old rocks from 65 million years ago, they find a lot of one type of rare metal called iridium. Because iridium is so rare on earth, it must have come from somewhere else like an asteroid. More evidence of this is from an enormous 180 kilometer (111 miles) wide crater in Mexico. It is called the Chicxulub Crater. An asteroid impact could have made such a crater.

(7)   A few scientists disagree with this explanation. They say that all this would cause dinosaurs to die much faster than they did. There are similar big craters around the world that affected ancient life.

Other Explanations
(8)   There could have been many large volcanic eruptions. Some scientists think that volcanic eruptions could have caused the K-T event. These volcanoes would release huge

amounts of ash and poisonous gases into the air. Like the dust in the asteroid explanation, this ash would stay in the air for a long time and cause acid rain.

(9)   These gases would also destroy the protective ozone layer in the sky. The ozone layer protects us from the sun's harmful rays.

(10)   Scientists have found out that there had been some huge eruptions. These eruptions could have covered both the states of Alaska and Texas with one kilometer of ash and lava!

7. Which explanation from the passage for why dinosaurs became is extinct is most convincing? Cite at least 3 pieces of evidence to support your explanation.

    _____

    _____

    _____

    _____

    _____

    _____

    _____

    _____

8. How is a cause and effect relationship about the extinction of dinosaurs shown in the third, fourth, and fifth paragraphs?

    _____

    _____

    _____

    _____

    _____

    _____

    _____

    _____

Directions: Read the rewritten passage of "Prehistory." Then answer questions 9-11.

Prehistory

What is Prehistory?

(1)   Prehistory means "before recorded history". History is what we know about the past as it has been recorded. Just like we still do today, people use to tell stories about the most interesting and challenging events in their people's lives even turning them into songs or family stories that were passed down from generation to generation. Later, stones, giant rock ledges and caves were scraped, chiseled, and even painted with drawings called petroglyphs. Petroglyphs could have been left for several reasons. It is possible that hunting parties or explorers left some drawings to help lead their people to safety They were also left to ward off intruders by giving an impression that the land here is off limits and protected by many gods or simply marking this valley a very successful hunting ground. These became very artistic in some regions and cultures.

(2)   Finally, about 6000 years ago people started to make marks on clay tablets to help them remember, and so writing was invented. Songs and tales likely were changed as they were learned by each new generation of musicians and storytellers. Painting and art usually only capture a moment in time, but writing can be used to describe everything in detail in past, present, and even what people expect for the future, like written laws, wills, and recorded deeds of land ownership. However, even though writing was a huge achievement for mankind, it took a very long time before it was used by everyone. At first not many people learned how to write, so history - our written record - really only emerged about 5000 years ago, in what we call The Bronze Age. That is why Historians (people who study history) don't know very much about what prehistoric people did.

(3)   The information we have about prehistoric people is mainly gathered from archeology - the art of finding and interpreting things that are buried in the ground. Sometimes we find ancient burial sites, which contain human remains and sometimes 'grave goods' which we can now date fairly accurately by measuring the decay on the artifact. Other such artifacts include weapons, jewelry, pottery, painting, even preserved post-holes and earth-works that allow us to imagine how their buildings may have looked and how they used to live.

(4)   Human activity really started when people picked up sticks and stones, bound them together and made themselves simple hammers, spears and other tools. Curiously, it seems that, because making and using tools is difficult to learn, language evolved to compliment simple grunts and gestures. This earliest period of truly human activity is known as the "Stone Age" which was followed by the "Bronze" and "Iron" Ages.

9. How does the author explain difficult words like "archeology" and "petroglyphs?" Cite 3 pieces of evidence to support your explanation.

_____

_____

_____

_____

_____

_____

_____

10. Compare and contrast prehistory with history. Explain your answer using at least 2 examples from the passage.

_____

_____

_____

_____

_____

_____

_____

11. The main idea of this passage is that artifacts and cave paintings helped historians learn about history and prehistory. How is the main idea revealed in the passage?

_____

_____

_____

_____

_____

_____

_____

_____

> **Directions**: Read the rewritten passage of "The Lumber Room." Then answer questions 12-13.

The Lumber Room

(1)   The children were to be driven, as a special treat, to the sands at Jagborough. Nicholas was not allowed to go because he was in trouble. Only that morning he had refused to eat his wholesome bread and milk on the crazy reason that there was a frog in it. Older and wiser people had told him that there could not possibly be a frog in his bread-and-milk and that he was not to talk nonsense. He continued, nevertheless, to talk what seemed like nonsense forever, and he described with much detail the color and markings of the frog. The dramatic part of the incident was that there really was a frog in Nicholas' bowl of bread-and-milk. He had put it there himself, so he obviously knew something about it. The problem of taking a frog from the garden and putting it into a bowl of wholesome bread-and-milk was exaggerated, but the fact that stood out the most according to Nicholas was that the older and wiser people had been proved to be profoundly about the frog in his bowl.

(2)   "You said there couldn't possibly be a frog in my bread-and-milk. There was a frog in my bread-and-milk," he repeated firmly.

(3)   So, his cousins and his quite uninteresting younger brother were to be taken to Jagborough sands that afternoon and he was to stay at home. His cousins' aunt, who insisted to invent the Jagborough expedition in order to make Nicholas sorry for his bad conduct at the breakfast-table. It was her habit, whenever one of the children was bad, to create something fun so that the bad child would be strictly forbidden to attend. However, if all the children were bad together, they were suddenly told of a circus in a neighboring town that they would not be allowed to attend that she had planned on taking them.

(4)   No tears fell from Nicholas's face when the time for trip came. As a matter of fact, however, all the crying was done by his cousin, who scraped her knee rather painfully against the step of the carriage as she was climbing in.

(5)   "How she did cry," said Nicholas cheerfully, as the party drove off without being happy.

(6)   "She'll soon get over that," said the aunt, "it will be a glorious afternoon for racing about over those beautiful sands. How they will enjoy themselves!"

(7)   "Bobby won't enjoy himself much, and he won't race much either," said Nicholas with a grim laugh because his boots are hurting him. They're too tight."

(8)   "Why didn't he tell me they were hurting?" asked the aunt sharply.

(9)   "He told you twice, but you weren't listening. You often don't listen when we tell you important things," said Nicholas.

(10)   "You are not to go into the gooseberry garden," said the aunt, changing the subject.

(11)   "Why not?" demanded Nicholas.

(12)   "Because you are in trouble," said the aunt proudly.

(13)   Nicholas felt perfectly capable of being in trouble and in a gooseberry garden at the same time. His face took on an expression of great stubbornness. It was clear to his aunt that he was determined to get into the gooseberry garden, "only," as she remarked to herself, "because I have told him he is not to."

(14)   Now the gooseberry garden had two doors by which it could be entered, and once a small person like Nicholas could slip in there he could disappear from view in the growth of artichokes, raspberry canes, and fruit bushes. The aunt had many other things to do that afternoon, but she spent an hour or two in unimportant gardening tasks among flower beds and shrubberies in order to keep a watchful eye on the two doors that led to the forbidden garden. She was a woman of few ideas but with great focus.

12. In what way is Nicholas negatively portrayed, due to his attitude about going to the Jagborough sands? Cite three pieces of evidence from the passage.

_____

_____

_____

_____

_____

_____

_____

_____

13. In an essay, explain how the trip to the Jagborough Sands affects the actions of Nicholas, the aunt, and the cousins.

Be sure to include:
*Nicholas's actions
*Aunt's actions
*Cousins' actions

_____

_____

_____

_____

_____

_____

_____

_____

_____

_____

_____

_____

_____

_____

_____

CONTINUE

Worksheet 3

Directions: Read the rewritten passage of "Rikki-tikki-tavi." Then answer questions 1-6.

Rikki-tikki-tavi

(1)   This is the story of the great problem that Rikki-tikki-tavi fought by himself in the bathrooms of the big bungalow in Segowlee military camp. Darzee, the tailorbird, helped him, and Chuchundra, the muskrat, who never comes out into the middle of the floor but always creeps round by the wall, gave him advice. However, Rikki-tikki did the real fighting. He was a mongoose which is rather like a little cat in his fur and his tail but quite like a weasel in his head and his actions. His eyes and the end of his nose were pink. He could scratch himself anywhere he pleased with any leg, front or back that he chose to use. He could fluff up his tail until it looked like a bottle brush. His war cry as he moved through the long grass was "Rikk-tikk-tikki-tikki-tchk!" One day a high summer flood washed him out of the burrow where he lived with his father and mother and carried him kicking and clucking down a roadside ditch. He found a little wisp of grass floating there and clung to it until he fell unconscious. When he woke up, he was lying in the hot sun on the middle of a garden path, very wet indeed, and a small boy was saying, "Here's a dead mongoose. Let's have a funeral."

(2)   "No," said his mother, "let's take him in and dry him. Perhaps he isn't really dead." They took him into the house, and a big man picked him up between his finger and thumb and said he was not dead but half choked. So, they wrapped him in cotton towel and warmed him over a little fire. He opened his eyes and sneezed.

(3)   "Now," said the big man, "don't frighten him, and we'll see what he'll do." He was an Englishman who had just moved into the bungalow. It is the hardest thing in the world to frighten a mongoose because he is completely curious. The motto of all the mongoose family is to run and find out, and Rikki-tikki was a true mongoose. He looked at the cotton towle, decided that it was not good to eat, ran all around the table, sat up, scratched himself, and jumped on the small boy's shoulder.

(4)   "Don't be frightened, Teddy," said his father.

(5)   Rikki-tikki looked down between the boy's collar and neck, sniffed at his ear, and climbed down to the floor where he sat rubbing his nose.

(6)   "Good gracious," said Teddy's mother, "and that's a wild creature! I suppose he's so tame because we've been kind to him."

(7)   "All mongooses are like that," said her husband. "If Teddy doesn't pick him up by the tail or try to put him in a cage, he'll run in and out of the house all day long. Let's give him something to eat." They gave him a little piece of raw meat. Rikki-tikki liked it a lot. When it was finished, he went out into the porch and sat in the sunshine and fluffed up his fur to make it dry. Then he felt better.

(8)   "There are more things to find out about in this house," he said to himself, "than all my family could find out in all their lives. I shall certainly stay and find out."

1. How does the flood affect the setting of the story?
    A. It changed the setting from the bungalow to another person's residence.
    B. It remained the same with Rikki Tikki Tavi being in the same bathroom.
    C. It changed back and forth between the bungalow and his friend's house.
    D. The flood caused Rikki Tikki Tavi to move to another country.

2. Based on the way Rikki Tikki Tavi's appearance is described in paragraph one, what conclusion can be drawn about the mongoose?
    A. He is difficult to detect what kind of animal he is.
    B. He was not a threat to anyone or anything.
    C. His reaction to certain actions could be problematic.
    D. He could be scary to others who didn't know him.

3. How did the father and son react differently when they saw Rikki-Tikki Tavi after the flood?
    A. The son wanted to bring the mongoose inside, but the father didn't want to help it.
    B. The father wasn't sure about the mongoose, but the son knew exactly what had happened to it.
    C. The father wanted to leave the mongoose on the side of the road, and the son wanted to bring him inside.
    D. The son thought the mongoose was dead, but the father wanted to try and save him.

4. What does the author suggessts about Rikki Tikki Tavi's condition in the following sentence from the passage? "He found a little wisp of grass floating there and clung to it until he fell unconscious."
    A. The mongoose was intelligent.
    B. The mongoose was wet.
    C. The mongoose was asleep.
    D. The mongoose was almost dead.

5. Think about the main idea of the passage. Which statement below would be included in a summary of the passage?
    A. The flood caused the mongoose to become unconscious.
    B. A mongoose finds a new home after a flood.
    C. The mongoose lived in a bungalow at the beginning of the story.
    D. A son was walking by the road when he saw the mongoose.

6. How do the actions of the characters suggest that the mongoose is a trusting and respectful animal?
    A.   Living in a bungalow, the family could trust the mongoose.
    B. The family takes in the animal even though the mongoose is a wild animal.
    C. The flood made the family feel sorry for the mongoose.
    D. Since the mongoose was found on the side of the street, he could be trusted.

Directions: Read the rewritten passage of "Pumas." Then answer questions 7-8.

Pumas

(1)   The puma or mountain Lion is a rather large cat though it is classified as a smaller cat by scientists. Like smaller cats, pumas cannot roar though they can muster a very startling snarl or a piercing cry. In some places, these cats are also called cougars, catamounts, painted cats, panthers or painters. Scientists call them puma concolor.

(2)   According to an old Mayan legend, all the animals of the jungle once looked the same until the gods offered to make them look different. The jaguar asked, "Let me be sprinkled with stars," and it was so. He was pleased with his gift and showed it to the puma. Not to be outdone, the puma asked the gods that he be as splendid as the jaguar, and it was so. Pleased with himself the puma went out to hunt. Unfortunately, he fell and rolled in the dust which clung to his still-wet design. For this foolishness he and all pumas afterwards went through life being the color of the ground.

Where do pumas live?

(3)   Pumas are widely spread in North, Central and South America. They can be seen in a variety of habitats including deserts, swamps and forests from northern British Columbia all the way down to the southern end of the Andes mountain range. Pumas were driven out of the eastern half of North America by human pressure. A small population remains in Florida and occasionally there are puma sightings in other eastern states. The puma's habitat looks mostly green or yellow depending on where they are in the world.

What do pumas look like?

(4)   Most pumas are a light brown color with black-tipped ears and tail. The pumas that live closest to the equator are the smallest and increase in size in populations closer to the poles. This increase is seen in tigers too. The smallest ones live in the tropics whereas the largest Siberian tigers live far to the north where winters are very cold. The endangered Florida Panther is the smallest of the pumas. Like many other cats, they can retract their sharp claws into their paws which have four toes. The largest male pumas can be as big as eight feet (2.4 meters) long, and females can be as large as seven feet (2.1 meters). The males weigh in a bit less than the average adult human at about 150 pounds (70 kilograms) with females weighing even less at 75 pounds (35 kilograms) or less.

(5)   Although pumas do not have a bright pattern, there are distinct black "tearstains" on their upper lips and a vivid white fur around the mouth that emphasizes facial expressions. Although cougars cannot roar, when they growl, they look rather intimidating.

7. Compare and contrast the way the way the puma's appearance is described in paragraph 4 to the legend about how the puma and jaguar got their appearance.

_____

_____

_____

_____

_____

_____

_____

8. Which key details are provided in the passage to support the idea that pumas are important animals to the cat family?

_____

_____

_____

_____

_____

_____

_____

Directions: Read the rewritten passage of "Earth." Then answer questions 9-11.

Earth

What is Earth?

(1)   Earth is the planet we live on. It is the only planet in the solar system with liquid water on its surface. It is also the only planet we know to have life on it. Earth is also known as Terra.

How big is the Earth?

(2)   The Earth is nearly 13,000 km wide. It's the largest terrestrial planet in the solar system. The Earth's mass is about 5,973,700,000,000,000,000,000,000 kg. That's a lot. But it is little compared with Jupiter (319 Earths) and tiny compared with the Sun (335,789 Earths) or other stars!

What is its surface like?

(3)   The Earth's surface is made of rock. Most of it is underwater but not all. Islands of rock rise up out of the water. The biggest islands are called continents of which there are seven: North America, South America, Europe, Asia, Africa, Australia, and Antarctica. The largest bodies of water are called oceans of which there are five: Pacific, Atlantic, Indian, Arctic and Antarctic or Southern.

(4)   The Earth's surface is made up of huge plates. They are like huge jigsaw pieces made of rock. These plates move very, very slowly, carrying the continents with them. They can rub beside each other, push against each other, or even move away from each other. If there are gaps between them, hot molten rock can rise up and make volcanoes. Where the plates rub or push against each other, earthquakes may happen. When two plates push each other's rock upwards, mountains are formed.

(5)   Earth has many kinds of environments. There are cold and icy places in Antarctica. There are hot and dry placed in deserts like the Sahara in Africa and Death Valley in the United States. There are cold and dry placed in deserts like Siberia in Russia. Where it is warm and wet, rainforests grow.

Why is there life on Earth?

(6)   Wherever we have looked on Earth, we have found living things. They may be very small, like bacteria, but they are there. We have found bacteria where it is very cold, very hot, very deep, very high or very dark.

(7)   What all living things on Earth seem to need is liquid water. Wherever you can find some water, there are almost always living things there too even if you can't see them. If we find liquid water somewhere else in the solar system, scientists think we might find some living things there too. If we don't, there is always the rest of the universe to explore!

(8)   There is another possibility. All the living things we know need liquid water. However, maybe somewhere else there are living things that don't need water. Perhaps we will need to learn how to recognize them.

What about the Earth's moon?

(9)   Earth has one moon. Sometimes it is called by its name in Latin, Luna, so we don't get confused with other planets and their moons. The moon has also been called Selene (pronounced "suh-LEE-nee") which is Greek for moon and was the name of the Greek moon goddess.

(10)   Recently we have also found some other objects that are said to go around the Earth. The largest one, called Cruithne (pronounced "cru-EE-nyuh"), is three miles wide. In fact, it orbits the sun in a way that makes it keep coming closer to Earth.

(11)   There are various ideas about where the moon came from, but the most widely held theory is that when the Earth was young, a large body hit the Earth and split off a section of the Earth that is now the moon.

9.   Describe the relationships between Earth and the moon and other objects that orbit it. Cite at least 3 pieces of evidence from the passage to support your description.

_____

_____

_____

_____

_____

_____

_____

_____

10. How does the author of the passage provide evidence to the idea that the huge plates that make up the continents can cause natural disasters?

_____

_____

_____

_____

_____

_____

11. In what ways does water play a vital role on Earth as well as the exploration of other living things?

_____

_____

_____

_____

_____

_____

Directions: Read the rewritten passage of "A Defenseless Creature." Then answer questions 12-13.

A Defenseless Creature

(1)   In spite of a suffering from arthritis during the night and the nervousness left by it, Kistunov went in the morning to his office and began punctually seeing the clients of the bank and persons who had come in with requests. He looked relaxed and exhausted and spoke in a faint voice hardly above a whisper as though he were dying.

(2)   "What can I do for you?" he asked a lady in an old cloak whose backside looked like a dung beetle.

(3)   "You see, your Excellency," the woman questioning began speaking rapidly, "my husband Shtchukin, a collegiate judge, was ill for five months and while he, if you will excuse my saying so, was bedridden at home. He was not dismissed from his job and when I went for his paycheck, they deducted twenty-four rubles thirty-six kopecks from his salary.

(4)   'What for?' I asked.

(5)   "He borrowed from the club fund," they told me, "and the other clerks had stood security for him. How was that? How could he have borrowed it without my permission? It's impossible, your Excellency. What's the reason of it? I am a poor woman, I earn my bread by taking in renters. I am a weak, defenseless woman, and I have to put up with cruelty from everyone and never hear a kind word."

(6)   The woman was blinking and dived into her cloak for her handkerchief. Kistunov took her request from her and began reading it.

(7)   "Excuse me, what's this?" he asked, shrugging his shoulders. "I can make nothing of it. Evidently you have come to the wrong place, madam. Your request has nothing to do with us at all. You will have to apply to the department in which your husband was employed."

(8)   "Why, my dear sir, I have been to five places already, and they would not even take the request anywhere," said Madame Shtchukin. "I'd quite lose my head, but, thank goodness my son-in-law, Boris Matveyitch, advised me to come to you. 'You go to Mr. Kistunov, Mamma because he is an influential man, and he can do anything for you' Help me, your Excellency!"

(9)   "We can do nothing for you, Madame Shtchukin. You must understand that your husband served in the Army Medical Department, and our establishment is a purely private commercial company. We are a bank. Surely you must understand that!"

(10)   Kistunov shrugged his shoulders again and turned to a gentleman in a military uniform with a swollen face.

(11)   "Your Excellency," piped Madame Shtchukin in a pitiful voice, " I have the doctor's certificate that my husband was ill! Here it is, if you will kindly look at it."

(12)   "Very good, I believe you," Kistunov said irritably, "but I repeat it has nothing to do with us. It's strange and positively absurd! Surely your husband must know where you are to apply?"

(13)   "He knows nothing, your Excellency. He keeps saying: 'It's not your business! Get away!' -- that's all I can get out of him. Whose business is it, then?"

(14)   Kistunov again turned to Madame Shtchukin and began explaining to her the difference between the Army Medical Department and a private bank. She listened attentively, nodded that she understood and said, "Yes . . . yes . . . yes . . . I understand, sir. In that case, your Excellency, tell them to pay me fifteen rubles at least! I agree to take part on account!"

12. In what way is the woman's behavior and manner of asking her request different from the way Kistunov is addressing the woman?

_____

_____

_____

_____

_____

_____

_____

13. In an essay, describe how the woman appears both aggressive and timid at the same time. Cite at least 3 pieces of evidence from the passage to support your ideas.

_____

_____

_____

_____

_____

_____

_____

_____

_____

_____

_____

_____

_____

_____

_____

_____

_____

_____

_____

_____

Worioksheet 4

Directions: Read the rewritten passage of "Rebecca of Sunnybrook Farm." Then answer questions 1-6.

Rebecca of Sunnybrook Farm

(1)   The old stage coach was rumbling along the dusty road that runs from Maplewood to Riverboro. The day was as warm as midsummer though it was only the middle of May, and Mr. Jeremiah Cobb was helping the horses as much as possible. Yet he never lost sight of the fact that he carried the mail. The hills were many, and the reins lay loosely in his hands as he laid back in his seat and extended one foot and leg luxuriously over the dashboard. His brimmed hat of worn felt was well pulled over his eyes, and he turned the wad of tobacco in his left cheek.

(2)   There was one passenger in the coach,--a small dark-haired person in a shiny tan calico dress. She was so slender and so stiffly starched that she slid from space to space on the leather cushions though she braced herself against the middle seat with her feet and extended her cotton-gloved hands on each side in order to maintain some sort of balance. Whenever the wheels sank farther than usual into a rut or jolted suddenly over a stone, she bounced into the air and came down again. She pushed back her funny little straw hat and picked up or selected more firmly a small pink sun shade which seemed to be her main duty to stay out of the sun. However, she would use her bead purse into which she looked whenever the conditions of the roads were not bumpy. She always found satisfaction in always looking at her precious contents in that purse so that she knew it neither disappeared nor grew less. Mr. Cobb never worried about the roads because his business was to carry people to their destinations and not necessarily to make them comfortable on the way. Indeed, he had forgotten about the girl in the back.

(3)   When he was about to leave the post office in Maplewood that morning, a woman came from a wagon, and coming up to him asked whether this was the Riverboro stage. She asked if he was Mr. Cobb. Answering in the affirmative, she nodded to a child who was eagerly waiting for the answer and who ran towards her as if she feared to be a moment too late. The child might have been ten or eleven years old perhaps, but whatever the number of her age, she had an appearance of being small for her age. Her mother helped her into the stage coach, paid the child's fare carefully and a put her bouquet of lilacs beside her.

(4)   All this had been half an hour ago, and the sun, the heat, the dust, the thought of doing errands in the great metropolis of Milltown, had lulled Mr. Cobb's lazy mind into complete forgetfulness as to his promise of keeping an eye on Rebecca.

(5)   Suddenly he heard a small voice above the rattle and rumble of the wheels and the creaking of the harness. At first, he thought it was a cricket, a tree toad, or a bird, but having determined the direction from which it came, he turned his head over his shoulder and saw a small shape hanging as far out of the window as safety would allow. A long black braid of hair swung with the motion of the coach. The child held her hat in one hand and with the other made attempts to poke the driver with her small sunshade.

1.   When the woman is "answering in the affirmative," what is happening?
   A.   Responding yes to a question
   B.   Responding no to a question
   C.   Ignoring a question
   D.   Asking a question back

2.   How does the description of the bumpy road reveal the driver's attitude?
   A.   It explains why the driver is grumpy and angry.
   B.   It describes the driver's attitude for being interested in his passengers.
   C.   It supports it since both are lazy and don't seem to care.
   D.   It contrasts the driver's helpful and concerned attitude.

3.   What does the girl do to try to get the driver's attention?
   A.   She doesn't do anything to get the driver's attention.
   B.   She yells at the driver.
   C.   She jabs at the driver.
   D.   She asks him a bunch of questions.

4.   How do you know that the young girl's ride is uncomfortable?
   A.   Because she continues to slide around in the seat
   B.   Because she mentions it to the driver
   C.   Because the driver tries to make the ride as uncomfortable as possible
   D.   Because the girl is young and small.

5.   In what way does the young girl show respect to the driver?
   A.   By helping the driver when the ride got bumpy
   B.   By paying for the ride in advance
   C.   By being polite when he speaks to her
   D.   By remaining silent so that the driver doesn't even know she is there

6.   Even though an emotion is not explicitly described, how does the girl most likely feel, based on her actions?
   A.   Content
   B.   Angry
   C.   Bothered
   D.   Odd

Directions: Read the rewritten passage of "Black Widows." Then answer questions 7-8.

Black Widows

(1)   A black widow is a shiny black spider. It has an orange or red mark that looks like an hourglass. Its abdomen is shaped like a sphere and has an hourglass mark on the bottom. Often there are just two red marks separated by black. Females sometimes have the hourglass shape on top of the abdomen above the silk-spinning organs called spinnerets. Females are usually about 1-1/2 inches long including their leg span. In areas where grapes grow, females are very small and round. They resemble shiny black or red grapes.

(2)   Male black widows are much smaller than females. Their bodies are only about 1/4 of an inch long. They can be either gray or black. They do not have an hourglass mark, but may have red spots on the abdomen.

(3)   Black widows are sometimes called "comb-footed" spiders. The bristles on their hind legs are used to cover trapped prey with silk.

(4)   Young spiders are called "spiderlings." They shed their outer covering known as an exoskeleton as they grow. Spiderlings are orange, brown, or white at first and get darker each time they shed their skin or molt.

(5)   The Latrodectus genus of black widow spiders is found throughout the world, especially where grapes grow. They live in North America, South America, and southern Europe. They are also found in Australia, New Zealand, and South Africa.

(6)   Their range in the United States is from Massachusetts to Florida, west to Texas, Oklahoma, Kansas, and California. They are most common in the southern states.

(7)   To catch prey, black widows build a "tangle" web. There are three distinct levels: supporting threads at the top, tangle threads in the middle, and vertical trap threads at the bottom. The trap threads are beaded with sticky droplets and attached to the ground. The black widow usually hangs upside down near the middle of the web. When a crawling insect breaks the ground attachment, the web lifts it up toward the waiting spider. Before the insect can get loose, the spider bites it and wraps it in silk.

(8)   The black widow's red or orange markings warn predators of danger. It is very quick and is able to detect small vibrations made by a predator. If threatened, it escapes down to the ground on a silk safety line. When disturbed, it often pretends to be dead.

(9)   The black widow's venom is poisonous. When fangs enter skin, they remain for several seconds. The venom glands are squeezed to deliver the poison through ducts in the fangs.

7.   Why is the hourglass shape mentioned several places in the first paragraph?

_____

_____

_____

_____

_____

_____

_____

_____

8. Even though this is an informative passage, how does the narrator create a mystifying and dangerous tone to the passage?

_____

_____

_____

_____

_____

_____

_____

_____

Directions: Read the rewritten passage of "Mound Builders." Then answer questions 9-11.

Mound Builders

(1)   The mound builders lived in what is today the eastern half of the United States and southern Canada in North America. Because the people who lived in these societies did not leave any written records, archaeologists look for similarities and differences between the mounds, and figure out which groups of mound builders interacted with each other. The name for this society comes from the fact that they left large earthen mounds behind in what appears to be community centers of activity. Many of these earthen mounds have been removed by modern people in North America, but they were found in many of the same locations where current cities in the United States are now located. They also lived in Spiro which is now present-day Oklahoma.

(2)   A major feature of most villages was a trading area where items could be exchanged for items that were made in places much more distant. It is known that these trading networks were quite large, and they may have even had contact with other major civilizations in North America like the Aztecs. Items such as knives have been found over 1000 miles from any known source of volcanic rock.

(3)   Often within these mounds, particularly some of the larger mounds, there have been the remains of what is assumed to be a major chief or king based on the items that were found buried with the person. This was also a reason for why many of these mounds have disappeared because early treasure hunters would dig through these mounds trying to find gold, silver, or other precious stones and jewelry.

(4)   They ate a wide variety of food items depending on where they were living. Corn (maize) was brought into the area from Mexico and was widely grown together with other vegetables like beans and squash. They also hunted both small animals like rabbits and squirrels and larger game animals like bison and various types of deer. In some lake regions, they ate wild rice and also ate fish either from the ocean or from freshwater lakes and rivers. They dried many foods to eat in the winter. They also drank water from freshwater rivers.

(5)   As far as we know, the mound builders never invented a written language with an alphabet. There are, however, images which have been carved into rocks and in caves as well as inscribed onto everyday objects like pottery. These can be found throughout North America. These images are called petroglyphs.

(6)   Often these symbols were arranged to tell a story or note something of significance to the people who drew these symbols. Usually these symbols would be used to remind a tribal elder about a story that would then be passed on to the next generation, and unless that oral history has been preserved, the story is usually lost.

(7)   The ceremonial masks, jewelry, and artifacts come from a wide range of places. The Hopewell mounds had copper from Lake Superior, mica from North Carolina, and shells from the Gulf Coast. This might show that the beliefs were held in a wide area, or it might only show that the

mound builders traded over a wide area. The first evidence of humans burying the dead comes from the mound builders.

(8)   We don't know the name of a single mound builder. Because the mound builders did not use writing, no names are known today. However, we are still researching them, and hopefully we will find names. There is some evidence (war, abandonment of some towns for small, stockaded settlements) that the civilization was in decline before the conquistadors arrived in Central America. The diseases brought by the conquistadors spread quickly through the Americas. Lots of people died from European diseases like smallpox, especially in Mississippian towns where people lived close together. By the time Europeans reached the Mississippi, many of the towns were empty.

(9)   They spread the cultivation of corn, beans, and squashes throughout Eastern and North America. These foods were the most important foods of many Native Americans, were important foods to the Europeans who settled the land, and are still important today. North Americans eat a lot of corn and beans. Some squashes (like pumpkins) are important symbols of fall and Thanksgiving in the US.

(10)   They left many mounds, which archeologists still study today. Some of the mounds are set aside in parks and monuments, so that people can look at the mounds, and learn from them. Some of the mounds are burial mounds which contain ornaments. Archeologists learn how people lived and dressed from what is left in the mounds. It is believed that they are the ancestors of several Native American Indian groups in North America.

9.   In what way are the mound builders similar to people today? The narrator includes some methods that mound builders used at that time. What methods are still in practice today?

_____

_____

_____

_____

_____

_____

_____

_____

10. Why do archaeologists have trouble learning about the mound builders? Cite 3 pieces of evidence from the passage to support your explanation.

_____

_____

_____

_____

_____

_____

_____

11. Describe the meaning of the word "inscribed" as it is used in the sentence below from the passage. Then explain how the author ensured that the reader would be able to figure out the meaning of this word.

There are, however, images which have been carved into rocks and in caves as well as inscribed onto everyday objects like pottery.

_____

_____

_____

_____

_____

_____

Directions: Read the rewritten passage of "The Dreamer." Then answer questions 12-13.

The Dreamer

(1)   It was the season of sales. The store of Walpurgis and Nettlepink had lowered its prices for an entire week as a discount much as an Arch-duchess might contract an attack of the flu for the unsatisfactory reason that the flu was locally accessible. Adela Chemping, who considered herself better than an ordinary bargain sale, made a point of attending the sale at Walpurgis and Nettlepink's.

(2)   "I'm not a bargain hunter," she said, "but I like to go where bargains are."

(3)   This showed that beneath her strength of character there was human weakness.

(4)   Mrs. Chemping had invited her youngest nephew to accompany her on the first day of the shopping expedition by throwing in a trip to the theater with light refreshments. As Cyprian was not yet eighteen she hoped he might not have reached that stage in his life when carrying her umbrella is looked on as repulsive.

(5)   "Meet me just outside the floral department," she wrote to him, "and don't be a moment later than eleven."

(6)   Cyprian was a boy who was a dreamer. He had the eyes of one who sees things that are not visible to ordinary people and sees the greater aspects in the common things in this world. He was quietly dressed, and his hair was brushed back in a smoothness as of ribbon seaweed. His aunt particularly noted this item when they met at the appointed place because he was standing waiting for her bare-headed.

(7)   "Where is your hat?" she asked.

(8)   "I didn't bring one with me," he replied.

(90   Adela Chemping was slightly upset.

(10)   "You are not going to be what they call a nut, are you?" she inquired with some anxiety, partly with the idea that a nut would refuse to carry parcels or umbrellas.

(11)   Cyprian looked at her with his wondering, dreamy eyes.

(12)   "I didn't bring a hat," he said, "because it is such a nuisance when one is shopping; I mean it is so awkward if one meets anyone one knows and has to take one's hat off when one's hands are full of umbrellas. If one hasn't got a hat on one can't take it off."

(13)   Mrs. Chemping sighed with great relief. Her worst fear had been laid at rest.

(14)   "It is normal to wear a hat," she observed, and then turned her attention briskly to the business in hand.

(15)   "We will go first to the table linen counter," she said, leading the way in that direction; "I should like to look at some napkins."

(16)   She wondered deeply about Cyprian as he followed his aunt. He belonged to a generation that is supposed to be focused on the role of a helper, but looking at napkins that one did not mean to buy was not a pleasure to him. Mrs. Chemping held one or two napkins up to the light and stared fixedly at them as though she half expected to find some secret message written on them in scarcely visible ink. Then she suddenly broke away in the direction of the glassware department.

    12. Describe the meaning of **nuisance** as it is used in paragraph 12. Next, explain how it further relates to both the aunt and to the nephew.

_____

_____

_____

_____

_____

_____

_____

_____

13. What is the importance of the young man wearing a hat and carrying the aunt's umbrella, and how does it contribute to the theme of the story? Cite 3 pieces of evidence from the passage to support your explanation.
Be sure to include:
*Aunt's thoughts about carrying her umbrella
*Nephew's thoughts about wearing a hat
*Differences between the two

_____

_____

_____

_____

_____

_____

_____

_____

_____

_____

_____

_____

_____

_____

_____

_____

_____

_____

_____

_____

_____

_____

_____

_____

_____

_____

_____

_____

_____

_____

_____

_____

_____

_____

_____

_____

Worksheet 5

Directions: Read the rewritten passage of "Transients in Arcadia." Then answer questions 1-6.

Transients in Arcadia

(1)   There is a hotel on Broadway that has not been discovered by the organizers of the summer vacation resort. It is deep and wide and cool. Its rooms are finished in dark oak. Homemade breezes and deep green shrubbery give it the beauty without having to deal with the problems of the Adirondack Mountains. One can climb its broad staircases or glide dreamily upward in its aerial elevators, attended by guides in brass button suits. There is a chef in its kitchen who will prepare for you brook trout better than the White Mountains ever served, seafood that would turn any top chef green with envy and Maine venison that would melt the official heart of a game warden.

(2)   A few have found out this beautiful place in the July desert of Manhattan. During that month you will see the hotel's few guests scattered about in the lofty dining room gazing at one another across the room of unoccupied tables silently.

(3)   Extra determined waiters hover nearby supplying everything we want before it is asked. The temperature is always like that in April. The ceiling is painted in water colors to fake a summer sky across which delicate clouds drift and do not vanish as those of nature.

(4)   The pleasing, distant roar of Broadway is transformed into the noise of a waterfall filling the woods with its restful sound. At every strange footstep the guests turn to see if their retreat has been discovered and invaded by the restless vacationers and residents who are forever trying to find nature.

(5)   Thus, in the nearly empty inn, the little band of vacationers jealously wait during the heated season so they can enjoy the delights of mountain and seashore that art been created for them.

(6)   In this July a woman came to the hotel whose card that she sent to the clerk for her name to be registered read "Mme. Heloise D'Arcy Beaumont."

(7)   Madame Beaumont was a guest that the Hotel Lotus loved. She possessed the fine appearance of the elite, tempered and sweetened by a graciousness that made the hotel employees bow down to her. Bell boys fought for the honor of answering her ring and the clerks would have given her the hotel and its contents. The other guests thought of her as the most beautiful and perfect woman.

(8)   This super excellent guest rarely left the hotel. To enjoy that wonderful inn, one must forego the city as though it were miles away. By night a brief trip up to the nearby roofs is in order, but during the sweltering day one remains in the empty inn.

1. How is the hotel on Broadway portrayed by the author's choice of words?
   A. As a hotel that has been around for a long time
   B. As the most relaxed and pleasant hotel
   C. As the crowded hotel with many amenities
   D. As a hotel with lots of arts and culture

2. In what way could this narrative be considered a fantasy as described in the example below?
   The pleasing, distant roar of Broadway is transformed into the noise of a waterfall filling the woods with its restful sound.
   A. If the figurative language was actually taking place in the story
   B. If the setting was taking place in the future
   C. Since the characters had supernatural powers
   D. Since the setting is in Manhattan

3. How does the few number of occupants in the inn contribute to the main idea of the story as this being a wonderful hotel to visit?
   A. The art culture of the hotel only attracts an artsy group of people.
   B. More people would rather stay at a better-known hotel than this one.
   C. Very few people know of this hotel because of its location in Manhattan.
   D. The hotel is so great that its customers want to keep it a secret.

4. What evidence supports the notion that Madame Beaumont was well-liked by everyone she came in contact with?
   A. "In this July a woman came to the hotel whose card that she sent to the clerk for her name to be registered read "'Mme. Heloise D'Arcy Beaumont'."
   B. "Bell boys fought for the honor of answering her ring"
   C. "She possessed the fine appearance of the elite,"
   D. "To enjoy that wonderful inn, one must forego the city as though it were miles away."

5. What does the author infer when she states "The ceiling is painted in water colors to fake a summer sky"?
   A. There really wasn't artwork on the ceiling, but there was the actual scene of the sky.
   B. The person who painted the artwork on the ceiling was not a real artist.
   C. The artwork on the ceiling should make people feel like they are there.
   D. A lovely artwork scene is on the ceiling by the guests painting it.

6. How does this hotel compare to other hotels in Manhattan?
   A. The best and most discreet hotel in Manhattan
   B. The worst hotel in Manhattan
   C. The least occupied hotel in Manhattan
   D. The most artistic hotel in the world

Directions: Read the rewritten passage of "Uranus." Then answer questions 7-8.

Uranus

(1)   Uranus, the seventh planet from the sun, was discovered by William Herschel on March 13, 1781. Uranus is 51,118 kilometers or about four Earths wide. It is the third widest and fourth heaviest planet in the solar system. Uranus does not have a surface that you could stand on without going deep into the atmosphere. Under the atmosphere, there may be an even mixture of rock and ice.

(2)   Uranus has eleven rings. They are dark in color and very hard to see. They were discovered by accident in 1977. Scientists were studying a bright star near Uranus. However, the star's light was blocked before and after it disappeared behind Uranus. From this, they figured out that Uranus has a ring system.

(3)   Uranus has 27 known moons which places it third in the solar system for the number of moons. The five main ones are Miranda, Ariel, Umbriel, Titania and Oberon.

(4)   Miranda is the smallest and closest of Uranus's major moons. It is mainly made of ice and rock. Miranda's surface has grooves, cliffs, and valleys. The moon was named after a character in The Tempest, a play by Shakespeare.

(5)   Ariel is made of rock and ice. Ariel has many valleys, but not many craters. Ariel was named after a character in the poem The Rape of the Lock by Alexander Pope. Ariel is also a spirit in The Tempest by Shakespeare.

(6)   Umbriel is made of lots of ices and some rock. It is also the darkest of Uranus's major moons. Umbriel was named after a character in the poem The Rape of the Lock by Alexander Pope.

(7)   Titania is the largest moon of Uranus. It is mostly ice and rock. The surface is covered with canyons. It was named after the Queen of the Fairies in A Midsummer's Night Dream, a play by Shakespeare.

(8)   Oberon is the outermost of the major moons of Uranus. It is made of the same things as Titania. It has many craters. Some of them have white rays around them and dark crater floors. It was named after the King of the Fairies in A Midsummer's Night Dream.

(9)   There are 13 tiny moons known to be orbiting Uranus inside Miranda's orbit. Nine more tiny moons are known to be in big orbits beyond Oberon's orbit.

(10)   One day on Uranus is about 17.24 Earth hours long. Uranus spins on its side, maybe because of a big impact early in the history of the solar system.

(11)   One year on Uranus would be 30,708 days or 84 years on Earth.

(12)   Uranus was named after Ouranos, the Greek name for the sky. Ouranos was the ancient Greek deity of the heavens, the earliest supreme God. According to Greek mythology, Ouranos was the husband and son of Gaia, Mother Earth.

7.   Describe why humans could not live on planet Uranus, according to the passage. Cite 3 pieces of evidence from the passage to support your description.

_____

_____

_____

_____

_____

_____

_____

_____

8. Typically, dramatic theatre performances from long ago do not tie in with the discovery of a planet. How does Shakespeare play a part in the discovery of Uranus?

_____

_____

_____

_____

_____

_____

_____

Directions: Read the rewritten passage of "Ants." Then answer questions 9-11.

Ants

(1)   Even though ants can look like small moving dots if you're standing, but when looking closely at an ant, you can see that it has antennae which are curved to look a lot like our own elbows. Ants also have small sharp claws that help them keep hold of things while moving around on objects such as trees.

(2)   Ants live in little "cities" called ant colonies. Ant colonies are found in many places including under stones, within living or dead wood, and even underground. More advanced ant species are great builders and create many chambers that are used for different reasons. A chamber may be used as a nursery or to store food. When ant colonies are underground, they are often covered with piles of dirt, sand, clay, or pine needles. These piles are called ant hills. Ant hills are used as entrances to the colony and as protection of the colony. Some ant hills are small, but others can grow as tall as 3 feet!

(3)   Depending on what type of species or role is in its ant colony, ants eat many different types of food. Species like the meat-eater ant eats mainly meat like the remains of dead animals but also can eat other foods including honey. Some other ant species, such as leafcutter ants actually "grow" their own food. They do this by collecting leaves and cutting them into pieces on which a type of fungus grows. The ants then harvest and eat this fungus.

(4)   Most ants work as a group to defend themselves. Whole colonies working together are sometimes called superorganisms, as the colony can act much like one large whole organism instead of the hundreds of tiny bugs that they really are. Another ant defense system is that some species of ants have venom which they could use for defense. This is also a reason why one particular species of ant is called a 'killer ant', even though these ants don't kill but can cause some damage to their victim.

(5)   Ants go through a type of metamorphosis called holometabolism which is a type of metamorphosis that includes a total of four stages. The ant begins life as an egg laid by the only reproducing female ant in an ant colony called a queen ant. After the egg hatches, it is in its baby stage which is called the larval stage. After a while, the ant larvae goes into a stage in which it cannot move and is also gaining its adult features. This stage is called the pupal stage. Finally, after a few weeks, the pupal casing the young ant was enclosed in is broken and the fully-adult ant comes out.

(6)   Most ants live up to 6 to 10 weeks with the exception of some queen ants which may live up to 15 years and some worker ants which may live up to 7 years.

(7)   Unlike many other animals, ants use smell instead of noises to talk to each other. Ants use a type of chemical called pheromones that leave a scent to help ants communicate, as well as figure out where each member of the colony is or was last located at. Ants also use their elbow-shaped antennae to smell as they don't have nostrils like humans have.

(8)   Ants can either help get rid of pests or be the pest itself. Ants can eat smaller insects that can be pests to a human's backyard or garden, but ants can also be pests as they can destroy some gardens. One species of ant known as the carpenter ant is sometimes a pest to humans because they eat wood. One kind of ant, the red imported fire ant, which is common in the southern United States, can deliver a very painful bite.

(9)   People in some parts of the world eat ants for food! Countries known for having dishes with ants on the menu include Mexico, Colombia and Thailand.

9. In what way is the passage organized so that the information about ants is relayed properly to the reader?

_____

_____

_____

_____

_____

_____

_____

10. How does the ant interact with humans, making them both beneficial and harmful to humans?

_____

_____

_____

_____

_____

_____

11. Why does the author include holometabolism in the passage and how does it play a role in the way ants mature and develop?

_____

_____

_____

_____

_____

_____

Directions: Read the rewritten passage of "A Tent in Agony." Then answer questions 12-13.

A Tent in Agony

(1)   Four men once came to a wet place in the forest to fish. They pitched their tent upon the pine-treed ridge of rocks in which a boulder could crash through the brush and whirl past the trees to the lake below. On the fragrant hemlock the fishermen slept unsuccessfully because the lake alternately the sun made them lazy and the rain made them wet. Finally, they ate the last bit of bacon and smoked and burned the last pancake.

(2)   Immediately a little man volunteered to stay and hold the camp while the remaining three should go to the Sullivan county to a farmhouse for supplies. They gazed at him miserably. "There's only one of you," they said in a final curse and disappeared down the hill in the known direction of a distant cabin. When it came to night, they had not returned. The little man sat close to his companion, the campfire, and stacked it with logs. He looked and believed to see a thousand shadows which were about to hurt him. Suddenly, he heard the approach of the unknown, crackling the twigs and rustling the dead leaves. The little man arose slowly to his feet and his pipe dropped from his mouth.

(3)   "Hah!" he bellowed hoarsely in danger. A growl replied and a bear walked into the light of the fire. The little man supported himself upon a sapling and looked at his visitor.

(4)   The bear was evidently a fighter because the black of his coat had become yellowish with age. There was confidence in his walk and arrogance in his small, twinkling eye. He rolled back his lips and disclosed his white teeth. The fire magnified the red of his mouth. The little man had never before confronted a terrible bear.

(5)   "Hah!" he roared. The bear interpreted this as a challenge. He approached warily. As he came near, the man became fearful. He cried out and then darted around the campfire.

(6)   "Ho!" said the bear to himself, "this thing won't fight because it runs. Well, suppose I will catch it." He started intensely around the campfire. The little man shrieked and ran furiously. Twice around they went.

(7)   In desperation the little man flew into the tent. The bear stopped and sniffed at the entrance. He scented the scent of many men. Finally, he ventured in.

(8)   The little man crouched in a distant corner. The bear advanced, creeping, his blood burning, his hair standing on end, and his jowls dripping. The little man yelled and rustled clumsily under the flap at the end of the tent. The bear snarled awfully and made a jump and a grab at his disappearing game. The little man, now without the tent, felt a tremendous paw grab his coat tails. He squirmed and wriggled out of his coat like a schoolboy in the hands of an avenger. The bear jerked the coat into the tent and took two bites, a punch and a hug before he, discovered his man was not in it. Then he grew not very angry. A bear on a spree is not a black-haired pirate. He is merely a troublemaker. He lay down on his

back, took the coat on his four paws and began to play with it. The most appalling, blood-curdling whoops and yells came to where the little man was crying in a treetop.

12. Why did the bear seem even more dangerous than an average bear, according to the passage? Cite 3 pieces of evidence from the passage to support your explanation.

_____

_____

_____

_____

_____

_____

_____

13. How are the personalities of the bear and the man displayed through their actions in the passage?
    Be sure to include:
    *personality of the bear
    *personality of the man
    *interaction between the two

_____

_____

_____

_____

_____

_____

_____

_____

_____

_____

_____

_____

_____

_____

_____

_____

Worksheet 6

Directions: Read the rewritten passage of "The Bag of Bagdad." Then answer questions 1-6.

The Bag of Bagdad

(1)   Without a doubt much of the spirit and intelligence of the Caliph Harun Al Rashid descended to the Margrave August Michael von Paulsen Quigg.

(2)   Quigg's restaurant is on Fourth Avenue which was a street that the city seems to have forgotten in the city's growth. Fourth Avenue was born and bred in the Bowery which meant it moved northward.

(3)   Where it crosses Fourteenth Street it struts for a brief moment proudly in the glare of the museums and cheap theaters. It is similar to the boulevard to the west or its other street to the east. It passes Union Square and here the hoofs of the horses seem to thunder in unison. Now comes the silent and terrible mountains--buildings square as forts, high as the clouds, shutting out the sky, where thousands of workers bend over desks all day. On the ground floors are only little fruit shops and laundries and book shops, where you see copies of "Littell's Living Age" and G. W. M. Reynold's novels in the windows. And next--poor Fourth Avenue!--the street becomes a silent street. On each side are shops devoted to "Antiques."

(4)   Let us say it is night. Antique knights in their rusty armor stand in the windows and threaten the passing cars with raised, rusty iron weapons. Here and there from a corner saloon stagger forth shuddering home-bound citizens moving down that Eldrich Avenue lined with the bloodstained weapons of the fighting dead in the antique stores. What street could live enclosed by these antiques.

(5)   This is not Fourth Avenue. It is not the tinsel but beauty of the Little Rialto and not after the echoing drum-beats of Union Square. There need be no tears, ladies and gentlemen. With a shriek and a crash Fourth Avenue dives headlong into the tunnel at Thirty-fourth and is never seen again.

(6)   Near the sad scene of the thoroughfare's ending stood the modest restaurant of Quigg. It stands there yet if you care to view its crumbling red-brick front, its show window heaped with oranges, tomatoes, layer cakes, pies, canned asparagus and its lobster and two Maltese kittens asleep on a bunch of lettuce, then you must. If you care to sit at one of the little tables upon whose cloth has been traced in the yellowest of coffee stains, then sit there with one eye on your umbrella.

(7)   One night at 9, at which hour the restaurant closed, Quigg set forth upon his quest. There was a mingling of the foreign, the military and the artistic in his appearance as he buttoned his coat high up under his short-trimmed brown and gray beard and turned westward toward the more central life of the city. Some called simply for a bowl of soup or sandwiches and coffee.

1. Why does the author compare "the silent and terrible mountains" to the buildings on the street?
    A. Because of their appearance
    B. Due to the way they are used
    C. Since they are so beautiful
    D. Because the buildings come to a peak

2.   How is Fourth Avenue compared to the other streets?
    A.   As inferior
    B. As superior
    C. Average
    D. In similar ways

3. How do the antiques described in paragraph four impact the rest of Fourth Avenue?
    A. As the only street that has antiques on them
    B. As haunting reminders
    C. As the highlight of the street
    D. As the only interesting thing on that street

4. What does the following line suggest in the passage about Fourth Avenue?
    With a shriek and a crash Fourth Avenue dives headlong into the tunnel at Thirty-fourth and is never seen again.
    A. The street widens before going into the tunnel.
    B. The ending of the street is at the tunnel.
    C. Many cars have crashed on this street
    D. The street passes straight through the tunnel.

5.   Why do the antique knights "threaten the passing cars with raised, rusty iron weapons" on Fourth Avenue?
    A. Because there are guards on Fourth Avenue who only allow certain people to pass
    B. Because they are ghosts on Fourth Avenue
    C. Because they face the street in the antique stores
    D. Because they are actual people in the costumes

6. How is Quigg restaurant described, compared to other stores on the other streets?
   A. As the restaurant with the most delicious food
   B. As an iconic restaurant in the city
   C. In an uplifting way
   D. In a depressing way

Directions: Read the rewritten passage of "Tigers." Then answer questions 7-8.

Tigers

(1)   Their speed and agility give the tiger the title of "Top Predator," over the larger but slower grizzly bear. The tiger is the largest and most powerful cat species living today. A well-rounded athlete, the tiger can climb (though not well), swim, leap great distances and pull with five times the force of a strong human. The tiger is in the same group (Genus Panthera) as lions, leopards, and jaguars. These four cats are the only ones who can roar. The tiger's roar is not like the full-voiced roar of a lion, but more like a sentence of snarly, shouted words.

(2)   Tigers live in forests and grasslands of eastern and southeastern Asia. They live in countries such as Bangladesh, Bhutan, China, India, Nepal, Cambodia, Laos, Malaysia, Myanmar, Thailand and Vietnam, Indonesia (Sumatra), and the Russian Far East. The Bengal Tiger is the national animal of Bangladesh and India.

(3)   Like the other big cats, tigers are built much like the much smaller domestic cats that people often have as pets. They are just much bigger and more powerful.

(4)   Tigers are usually orange or reddish orange with very bold, uneven black stripes and white areas on the chest, neck, belly and inside of the legs. Their stripes act as camouflage, making it difficult for them to be seen when they are among the trees and shrubs of the jungle. The stripes will vary with each individual tiger.

(5)   A tiger usually is about 6 ft to 9 ft in length from nose to tail tip. A large tiger might be 10 ft (3 meters) long. The tail is about 36 inches (91 cm or 3 ft). Tigers weigh about 350 to 550 pounds (160 to 250 kg).

(6)   Tigers have very strong teeth and jaws. Their paws are soft and heavily padded, sheathing large, very sharp claws. They also have short, thick, and soft fur and thick long whiskers.

(7)   White tigers are those who are born with a certain genetic defect causing loss of pigment in their skin, eyes and fur. These tigers can be white with black, grey, very dark blue, or no stripes. However, they are not albino.

(8)   Tigers mostly feed on plant-eaters, or herbivores, like elk, deer, wild pigs, and buffalo. Like the majority of cats, they are solitary hunters, meaning they hunt alone. When a tiger has spotted its prey, it may seek out a good location where it can hide, staying close to the ground, and wait for the perfect moment to pounce and ambush its prey. When prey becomes scarce

tigers also hunt peacocks and rabbits. Resourceful as they are, they also catch and eat fish, as tigers are good swimmers.

(9)   People who traditionally live in areas where tigers hunt have learned to avoid tiger attacks by wearing a face-mask on the backs of their heads. Tigers prefer to approach other animals from behind and think twice about pouncing when they can see a face. Fortunately, they rarely attack humans unless they are too ill to hunt their normal prey. Tigers that attack humans are called man-eaters. Jim Corbett was a famous hunter and conservationist who killed many man-eating tigers in India.

7.   According to the passage, what can people do to avoid getting attacked by a tiger?

_____

_____

_____

_____

_____

_____

_____

_____

8. The main idea of the passage is about the strength of a tiger. How is this idea conveyed in the passage with key details?

_____

_____

_____

_____

_____

_____

_____

_____

Directions: Read the rewritten passage of "Danish Kings." Then answer questions 9-11.

Danish Kings

(1)   Sweyn Haraldssen was born in Denmark around the year 960. His nickname is "Forkbeard" which is a nickname that probably was used during his lifetime and refers to a long, pitchfork-like moustache rather than a full beard. Such a moustache was fashionable at the time, particularly in England. Sweyn succeeded his father, Harold I "Blåtand" (Bluetooth), as king of Denmark probably in late 986 or early 987. Following the death of Norway's King Olaf I Tryggvason in the Battle of Svolder in 1000, Sven established Danish control over most of Norway.

(2)   Sweyn was almost certainly involved in the raids against England in 1003 to 1005, 1006 to 1007, and 1009 to 1012, following the massacre of England's Danish inhabitants in November 1002 during the reign of Ethelred the Unready. Sven is thought to have had a personal interest in these due to his sister, Gunhilde, being amongst the victims. Sven acquired massive sums of Danegeld as a result of the raids, and in 1013 personally led the Danish fleet in a full-scale invasion.

(3)   The Laud Chronicle says that "before the month of August came king Sweyn with his fleet to Sandwich. He went very quickly about East Anglia into the Humber's mouth, and so upward along the Trent till he came to Gainsborough. Eorl Uhtred and all Northumbria quickly bowed to him, as did all the folk of Lindsey, then the folk of the Five Boroughs. He was given hostages from each shire. When he understood that all the people had submitted to him, he ordered that his force should be provisioned and horsed. He went south in full force, and entrusted his ships and the hostages to his son Canute. After he came over Watling Street, they worked the most evil that a force might do. They went to Oxford, and the town-dwellers soon bowed to him, and gave hostages. From there they went to Winchester, and did the same."

(4)   However, when he came to London, the Londoners destroyed the bridges that spanned the River Thames. It is this action that is referred to in the song London Bridge is Falling Down. Sweyn suffered heavy losses and had to withdraw. King Sweyn then went to Wallingford, over the Thames to Bath, and stayed there with his troops. The leading noblemen there all bowed to Sweyn and gave hostages. London withstood the assault of the Danish army, but the city was now alone. King Ethelred the Unready fled to Normandy in late 1013. With the acceptance of the Anglo-Saxon council, the Witan, London finally surrendered to Sweyn, and he was declared "king" on Christmas Day.

(5)   Sweyn based himself in Gainsborough, Lincolnshire and began to organize his vast new kingdom, but he died there on 3 February 1014, having ruled England unopposed for only five weeks. His body was later returned to Denmark and buried at Roskilde Cathedral. He was succeeded as King of Denmark by his eldest son with his wife Gunhilde. The Danish fleet proclaimed his younger son Canute as King of England, but they and he returned to Denmark, and Ethelred the Unready became King of England again.

9.   How was King Sweyn Haraldssen characterized as a violent king throughout the passage?

_____

_____

_____

_____

_____

_____

_____

_____

10. What role did hostages play in the reign of King Sweyn Haraldssen?

_____

_____

_____

_____

_____

_____

_____

_____

11. How did the song "London Bridge is Falling Down" come to be from the historical events of the Danish king?

_____

_____

_____

_____

_____

_____

_____

_____

Directions: Read the rewritten passage of "Two Military Executions." Then answer questions 12-13.

Two Military Executions

(1)   In the spring of the year 1862 General Buell's big army lay in camp getting itself into shape for the campaign which resulted in the victory at Shiloh. It was a raw, untrained army, although some of its soldiers had seen hard enough service with a good deal of fighting in the mountains of Western Virginia and in Kentucky. The war was young and soldiering a new industry, imperfectly understood by the young American of the period, who found some features of it not altogether to his liking. Chief among these was that essential part of discipline, subordination. Private Bennett Story Greene committed the carelessness of striking his officer. He was promptly arrested on complaint of the officer, tried by court-martial and sentenced to be shot.

(2)   "You might have thrashed me and let it go at that," said the condemned man to the complaining witness, "that is what you used to do at school, when you were plain Will Dudley and I was as good as you. Nobody saw me strike you and discipline would not have suffered much."

(3)   "Ben Greene, I guess you are right about that," said the lieutenant. "Will you forgive me? That is what I came to see you about."

(4)   There was no reply, and an officer putting his head in at the door of the guard-tent where the conversation had occurred, explained that the time allowed for the interview had expired. The next morning, when in the presence of the whole brigade Private Greene was shot to death by a squad of his comrades, Lieutenant Dudley turned his back upon the sorry performance and muttered a prayer for mercy, in which he himself was included.

(5)   A few weeks afterward, as Buell's leading division was being ferried over the Tennessee River to assist in helping Grant's beaten army, night was coming on, and it was black and stormy. Through the wreck of battle the division moved, inch by inch, in the direction of the enemy, who had withdrawn a little to reform his lines. But for the lightning the darkness was absolute. Never for a moment did it cease, and ever when the thunder did not crack and roar were heard the moans of the wounded among whom the men felt their way with their feet, and upon whom they stumbled in the gloom. The dead were there, too--there were dead a-plenty.

(6)   In the first faint gray of the morning, when the swarming advance had paused to resume, something of a line of battle and skirmishers had been thrown forward. Word was passed along to call the roll. The first sergeant of Lieutenant Dudley's company stepped to the front and began to name the men in alphabetical order. He had no written roll, but a good memory. The men answered to their names as he ran down the alphabet to G.

(7)   "Gorham." "Here!" "Grayrock." "Here!" The sergeant's good memory was affected by habit: "Greene." "Here!" The response was clear, distinct, unmistakable!

(8)   A sudden movement, an agitation of the entire company front, as from an electric shock, proved the startling character of the incident. The sergeant paled and paused. The captain strode quickly to his side and said the name sharply.

(9)   All faces turned in the direction of the familiar voice. The two men between whom in the order of stature Greene had commonly stood in line turned and squarely confronted each other.

(11)   "Once more," commanded the investigator, and once more came the name of the dead man: "Bennett Story Greene." "Here!"

(12)   At that instant a single rifle-shot was heard away to the front and beyond the skirmish-line with a full stop the captain's exclamation, "What the devil does it mean?"

(13)   Lieutenant Dudley pushed through the ranks from his place in the rear. "It means this," he said, throwing open his coat and displaying a visibly broadening stain of crimson on his breast. His knees gave way, and he fell awkwardly and lay dead.

(14)   A little later the regiment was ordered out of line to relieve the congested front, and through some misplay in the game of battle was not again under fire. Nor did Bennett Greene, expert in military executions, ever again signify his presence at one.

12. Describe the ironic instance that takes place during roll call when Private Greene's name is called.

_____

_____

_____

_____

_____

_____

_____

_____

13. How did Private Greene's attitude toward his actions and his execution change throughout the course of the passage?

Be sure to include:

*his attitude at the beginning of the story

*his attitude right before the execution

*his attitude after the execution

_____

_____

_____

_____

_____

_____

_____

_____

_____

_____

_____

_____

_____

_____

CONTINUE

Worksheet 7

According to Their Lights

(1)   Somewhere in the depths of the big city where the loud neighborhoods are forever being shaken together, young Murray and the Captain had met and become friends. Both were at their lowest financially. Both were striving to make some money after graduating from college.

(2)   The captain was no longer a captain. One of those sudden actions from a high and profitable position in the Police Department where he would rip off his badge and buttons and decided to try his hand at real estate so that he could make some more money. The passing of the flood left him low and dry. One month after his problem, a saloon-keeper plucked him by the neck from his free-lunch counter as a tabby plucks a strange kitten from her nest and threw him out of the lunch counter and onto the asphalt. This seems low enough. However, after that he wrote complaining letters to the newspapers. Then he fought the attendant at the Municipal Lodging House who tried to give him a bath. When Murray first saw him, he was holding the hand of an Italian woman who sold apples and garlic on Essex street, and quoting the words of a song book ballad.

(3)   All the pretty things of Gotham had once been his. The house of his uncle was always observed on the grand and revered avenue.

(4)   One evening the former Captain and young Murray sat on a bench in a little downtown park. The great bulk of the Captain which starvation seemed to increase lay against the arm of the bench in a shapeless mass. His red face, week-old whiskers and topped by a sagging white straw hat looked in the gloom like one of those structures that you may observe in a dark window. A tight-drawn belt was the last possession of the Captain's former years. The Captain's shoes were buttonless.

(5)   Murray, at his side, was shrunk into his dingy and ragged suit of blue serge. His hat was pulled low. He sat quiet and a little indistinct like some ghost that had been dispossessed. "I'm hungry," growled the Captain, "and I'm starving to death. Right now, I could eat a Bowery restaurant clear through to the stovepipe in the alley. Can't you think of nothing, Murray? You sit there with your shoulders scrunched up. Think of some place we can get something to chew."

1. **The passing of the flood left him low and dry.**
   Consider the sentence above from the passage. How did this hurt the young Captain financially?
   A. The flooding caused so much damage to his house that he couldn't afford to keep his house.
   B. The former Captain wasn't getting paid from his real estate business.
   C. In real estate, the water must have flooded the houses that he was trying to sell.
   D. The former Captain got fired from his duty on the police force.

2. For what reason did the man make a change in his career from Police Captain to real estate agent?
   A. Because he was shot while on the police force
   B. Because he wanted to make more money
   C. Because he hated being a police officer
   D. Because someone talked him into working in real estate

3. Based on the description of the former Captain in paragraph 2, how could the former captain be categorized?
   A. Teacher
   B. Homeless person
   C. Minimum-wage worker
   D. Laborer

4. When did young Murray first see the former Captain and realize his financial situation?
   A. At young Murray's house
   B. On a downtown park bench
   C. When he was selling apples on the street to an Italian woman
   D. When the former Captain was trying to get a woman to give him food

5. After the first paragraph, how do you infer that young Murray is in a similar financial situation as the young Captain?
   A. Because young Murray was sleeping on the streets
   B. By the way that young Murray walked
   C. His clothing is described as being someone who is in financial need
   D. Murray explains his financial problem to the former Captain.

6. Besides young Murray, how did the other characters in the street treat and interact with the former Captain?
   A. With sympathy
   B. As if he was nobody
   C. As the Captain of the police department
   D. As a rich person

Directions: Read the rewritten passage of "Oort Clouds." Then answer questions 7-8.

Oort Clouds

(1)   Scientists say there is a distant group of objects made of rock and ice that forms a cloud-like region surrounding our solar system. It is a cloud of comet-like objects orbiting far away from the sun. Even though the comets are very widely scattered from each other, there are many millions of them. The total mass of all these comets may be up to 100 times the mass of the Earth. The Oort Cloud is named after a Dutch astronomer Jan Oort who took the original idea, improved upon it and made it widely known.

(2)   As a comet makes several passes through the solar system, the sun slowly melts and vaporizes the ice and only little bits of solid debris are left behind. If the comets are all destroyed when they pass through the system, then new comets will need to appear. Otherwise we would not see any more comets. Jan Oort used the idea of the Oort cloud to explain why new comets keep appearing.

(3)   If you can imagine the distance from the Earth to the sun, then the comets in the Oort cloud are 50,000 to 100,000 times further away! That is 1,000 times further away from the sun than is Pluto and about one fourth the distance to the nearest neighboring star—Proxima Centauri. Light takes a year to travel from the sun to the outer edge of the Oort Cloud.

(4)   The Oort cloud objects may have started closer to the sun during the solar system's formation. When they passed near the gas giants, the gravity of those planets hurled the objects into very distant orbits. The Oort cloud objects were sent in all directions, making the Oort cloud ball-shaped instead of disk-shaped. The gravity of passing stars also made the orbits of these objects more circular, and pulled them further from the sun. Sometimes the gravity of other far away stars can send the objects hurtling back toward the sun. These become the comets.

(5)   An object named Sedna has been discovered that may belong to the Oort Cloud (although it is actually between the Kuiper Belt and the Oort Cloud.) It is from 1,180 to 1,800 km across. Its orbit stretches from 76 to 928 times further from the sun than does the Earth's. Sedna orbits the sun about once every 11,250 Earth years. The last time Sedna was where it is now in its orbit, Earth's last Ice Age was ending! Some scientists think that Sedna should be included in the Kuiper Belt, making the belt bigger.

7. Describe the location of the Oort Clouds and the significance of the objects that are found within them.

_____

_____

_____

_____

_____

_____

_____

8. How were the Oort Clouds discovered by a scientist?

_____

_____

_____

_____

_____

_____

_____

Directions: Read the rewritten passage of "The Romans." Then answer questions 9-11.

The Romans

(1)   At the start, the Romans lived in a region that now forms part of Italy. Through conquest of nearby people, the Roman Empire expanded. At its peak, the empire controlled most of Western Europe, North Africa, Greece, the Balkans, and the Middle East. The capital Rome grew from a simple village to a thriving metropolis. Even today, some 2500 years later, Rome is still a major world city.

(2)   Remains of the top floors of a building are near the Capitolium and the Aracoeli in Rome. Many public buildings built by the Romans were huge works of white marble complete with arches and grand architecture. The average house, by comparison, was smaller and plainer being built of bricks and timber. Much of our extensive knowledge of Roman buildings comes from ruins and remains left in the ground.

(3)   Inside a middle class home (a domus), there were many rooms, with distinct functions. These ranged in size, from small cubicles in which they slept through medium sized rooms in which they ate to large halls in which they would receive and entertain guests. The rooms in the house normally opened out onto a courtyard. Despite its often small size, the purpose of this courtyard was to provide light and air to the rooms. As well as a courtyard, most wealthy people would also have kept a garden behind the house in which flowers, fruit, vegetables, and even grape vines would have been grown.

(4)   In the city of Rome most people lived in two or three-story apartment buildings called Insulae. Here a whole family lived in only one or two rooms spending much of their time outside in the courtyards and streets. Water came from nearby public fountains and aqueducts.

(5)   The Romans also constructed many public buildings including temples, marketplaces, forum, and amphitheaters. These public works also included things required for city living like aqueducts and sewers.

(6)   Military buildings were also undertaken, the largest construction being Hadrian's Wall at the northern fringes of the Roman Empire. Even today, the remains of these roads are still visible in Northern England.

(7)   At its pinnacle, the Roman Empire covered much of Europe, northern Africa, and some of the Middle East. There are many different ethnicities in these regions. Some of them are the direct descendants of Roman citizens while other people and ethnicities emerged through immigration into these areas from other regions. In Rome, the capital city of the Roman Empire, there are currently Italian people who have a blend of Roman heritage and other people that emigrated to the area after the Roman Empire dissolved.

(8)   Many modern European languages have evolved from Latin, the language of the Roman Empire. These are called Romance languages, and they include Italian, Spanish, and French. Today Romance languages are also spoken in many countries in South America and Africa.

9.   In what way was the Roman life a simple life for those who lived in ancient civilization? Cite 3 pieces of evidence from the passage to support your explanation.

_____

_____

_____

_____

_____

_____

_____

_____

10. How were the rooms in Roman houses different for people of different socioeconomic statuses?

_____

_____

_____

_____

_____

_____

_____

_____

11. How can people today experience what Rome was like 2500 years ago?

_____

_____

_____

_____

_____

_____

_____

Directions: Read the rewritten passage of "The Snake." Then answer questions 12-13.

The Snake

(1)   Where the path wound across the ridge, the bushes of huckleberry and sweet fern swarmed at it in two curling waves until it was a mere winding line traced through a tangle. A man and a dog came from the laurel thickets of the valley where the white brook moved with the rocks. They followed the deep line of the path across the ridges. The dog, a large lemon and white setter, walked tranquilly at his master's heels.

(2)   Suddenly from some unknown and yet near place there came a dry, shrill whistling rattle that instantly trembled the limbs of the man and the dog. Like the fingers of sudden death, this sound seemed to touch the man at the nape of the neck, at the top of the spine, and change him as swift to a statue of listening horror. The dog too stood crouched and quivering. His jaw dropping, and the froth of terror upon his lips.

(3)   Slowly the man moved his hands toward the bushes, but his glance did not turn from the place that made sinister by the warning rattle. His fingers sought for a stick of weight and strength. Presently they closed around one that seemed adequate, and holding this weapon poised before him the man moved slowly moved forward. The dog with his nervous nostrils fairly fluttering moved warily, one foot at a time, after his master.

(4)   But when the man came upon the snake, his body underwent a shock. With a white face, he sprang forward and his breath came in strained gasps, his chest heaving. His arm with the stick made a defensive gesture.

(5)   The snake had apparently been crossing the path in some travel when to his sense there came a person. The dull vibration perhaps informed him, and he flung his body to face the danger. He had no knowledge of paths. He had nothing to tell him to slink noiselessly into the bushes. He knew that his enemies were approaching and no doubt they were seeking him and hunting him. So he cried his cry.

(6)   "Beware! Beware! Beware!"

(7)   The man and the snake confronted each other. In the man's eyes were hatred and fear. In the snake's eyes were hatred and fear. These enemies maneuvered, each preparing to kill. It was to be a battle without mercy. Neither knew of mercy for such a situation.

(8)   As for this snake in the pathway, there was a double curve some inches back of its head, which made the man feel the death-fingers at the nape of his neck. The reptile's head was waving slowly from side to side and its hot eyes flashed. Always in the air was the dry, shrill whistling of the rattles.

(9)   "Beware! Beware! Beware!"

(10)   The man made the first movement with his stick. Instantly the snake's heavy head and neck were bended back on the double curve and instantly the snake's body shot forward in a low, hard spring. The man jumped and swung his stick. The blind, sweeping blow fell upon the snake's head and hurled him. He rallied swiftly, agilely, and again the head and neck bended back to the double curve, and the steaming, wide-open mouth made its desperate effort to reach its enemy. This attack, it could be seen, was despairing, but it was nevertheless ferocious of the same quality.

12. Did the dog help or hinder the man's chances of winning the battle against the snake? Explain your reasoning.

_____

_____

_____

_____

_____

_____

_____

_____

13. Describe the plan for winning the battle from the snake's point of view and the man's point of view. Explain which one has the better plan for winning.
Be sure to include:
*the snake's plan
*the man's plan
*the best plan

_____

_____

_____

_____

_____

_____

_____

_____

_____

_____

_____

_____

_____

_____

CONTINUE

TEST 1

Total Points: 100

> **Directions**: Read the rewritten passage of "Doctor Chevalier's Lie." Then answer questions 1-6.

Doctor Chevalier's Lie

(1)   The quick sound of a pistol rang through the quiet autumn night. It was no unusual sound in the unpleasant area where Dr. Chevalier had his office. Screams commonly went with it. This time there had been none.

(2)   Midnight had already rung in the old cathedral tower.

(3)   The doctor closed the book over which he had lingered so late and awaited the order that was almost sure to come.

(4)   As he entered the house to which he had been called he could not but note the frightening detail that accompanied these recurring events. The same scurrying; the same groups of frightened women bending over banisters while being hysterical. Some of them were morbidly curious, and others were shedding tears. A dead girl stretched out as they always were.

(5)   Yet it was not the same. Certainly, she was dead. There was the hole in the temple where the bullet went through. Yet it was different. Other such faces had been unfamiliar to him, but they resembled the same encounter of a loved one dying. This one was not.

(6)   Like a flash he saw it again amid other surroundings. The time was little more than a year ago. The place, a homely cabin down in Arkansas, in which he and a friend had found shelter and hospitality during a hunting expedition.

(7)   There were others beside. A little sister or two and a father and mother were upset, but they were proud as angels of their girl, who was too clever to stay in an Arkansas cabin, and who was going away to seek her fortune in the big city.

(8)   "The girl is dead," said Doctor Chevalier. "I knew her well and charge myself with her remains and decent burial."

(9)   The following day he wrote a letter. One letter carried sorrow, but no shame to the cabin down there in the forest.

(10)   It told that the girl had sickened and died. A lock of hair was sent and other trifles with it. Tender last words were even invented.

(11)   Of course, it was believed that Doctor Chevalier had cared for the remains of a woman of low standing.

(12)   Shoulders were shrugged. Society thought of firing him. Society did not, for some reason or another, so the event blew over.

1. How does the flashback of Dr. Chevalier's hunting expedition play a role in the actual story? (3 POINTS)
    A. Sympathy felt during the flashback is felt again by Dr. Chevalier with the new death.
    B. It provides a similarity between the feelings expressed by both families of the deceased.
    C. The family had experienced an earlier death in the family.
    D. Dr. Chevalier met a family with contrasting feelings when someone died in their family.

2. What seemed different in the visit by Dr. Chevalier at the beginning of the story? (3 POINTS)
    A. The people were acting somewhat different about the dead girl.
    B. The dead girl had died in a different manner than suspected.
    C. The family was unaware that the girl had died.
    D. The family was speaking oddly about the deceased.

3. What does the following statement about Dr. Chevalier after writing the letter reveal about his character? (3 POINTS)
    Tender last words were even invented.
    A. He didn't feel sympathy for the deceased.
    B. He felt bad for the person who died and their family.
    C. He wanted to help the family as best as he could.
    D. He really did not know what to say.

4. What does the phrase "so the event blew over" mean in regards to what was happening to Dr. Chevalier when "society thought of firing him"? (3 POINTS)
    A. The town would wait to fire Dr. Chevalier later.
    B. Dr. Chevalier was fired for this event.
    C. The town waited for the townspeople to stop thinking about the event.
    D. A terrible crime took place and the town wanted to make sure that everyone knew about it.

5. What evidence in the passage best supports that Dr. Chevalier was a thoughtful doctor?
   (3 POINTS)
   A. "Tender last words were even invented."
   B. "I knew her well and charge myself with her remains and decent burial."
   C. "It told that the girl had sickened and died."
   D. "it was believed that Doctor Chevalier had cared for the remains of a woman of low standing."

6. What description best explains where Dr. Chevalier's office was located in the city?
   (3 POINTS)
   A. In a crime-infested part of town
   B. In a suburb
   C. On the outskirts of town
   D. On a quiet street

> **Directions**: Read the rewritten passage of "Babylonians." Then answer questions 7-8.

Babylonians

(1)   The Babylonians were based in what is now modern-day Iraq. They controlled much of the land between the rivers of the Tigris and the Euphrates. They were the last of a string of city states (civilizations based around a single powerful city) to control this area.

(2)   In the 24th century BC the city of Babylon was founded on the banks of the river Euphrates. In the 18th century BC it became a capital of Babylonian empire.

(3)   Babylon reached its glory in 6th century BC. Constructions like Ishtar Gate and Etemenanki ziggurat were built, making Babylon the most beautiful city of the ancient world.

(4)   Ishtar Gate was one of the eight gates of the Babylon city. Dedicated to the goddess Ishtar, the Gate was constructed of blue glazed tiles with alternating rows of relief dragons and bulls. The roof and doors of the gate were of cedar. Through the gate ran the Processional Way, which was lined with walls covered in lions on glazed bricks (about 120 of them). Statues of the gods were paraded through the gate and down the Processional Way each year during the New Year's celebration.

(5)   Processional Way led to Etemenanki ziggurat. A ziggurat was a pyramid-like tower that they made for their gods. Etemenanki was seven stories, or 91 meters high, and had a temple of Marduk on top of it. Ishtar Gate is currently displayed in Pergamon Museum in Berlin. Only ruins are left of Etemenanki ziggurat.

(6)   The Babylonians ate melons, plums, prunes and dates. Barley was their staple crop that they would make flat breads with. The bread would then be eaten with some fruit. For meat they ate pork, poultry, beef, fish and mutton (sheep meat). Onions and garlic were common seasonings for their food. Babylonians didn't drink wine, but instead they drank beer made out of barley.

(7)   One of Babylon's most famous kings was Hammurabi. He ruled for 43 years. Hammurabi is famous for creating one of the first formal written set of laws. These laws were written on a stone tablet standing over six feet tall. The most famous rule he set is now known as an eye for an eye. This rule said that the punishment for lawbreakers would be the same as the crime they committed. So, if a criminal stabbed a person in the eye, the criminal would be stabbed in the eye too. The laws he made were known as "The Code Of Hammurabi". This legal system was spread throughout Asia and Europe. The Code of Hammurabi is also interesting because it was the first set of laws which presumed people were innocent, meaning a person must be proven guilty before they could be punished for their crimes.

(8)   Nebuchadnezzar II is mentioned in The Bible (The Christian holy book), the Torah (The Jewish holy book) and the Qur'an (The Islamic holy book). He was a ruler of Babylon who destroyed the Jewish temples in Jerusalem.

7. How did Hammurabi become part of the Babylonian history? (10 POINTS)

_____

_____

_____

_____

_____

_____

_____

8. Why is Ishtar Gates popular in the Babylonian history and culture? (10 POINTS)

_____

_____

_____

_____

_____

_____

_____

Directions: Read the rewritten passage of "Fireflies." Then answer questions 9-11.

Fireflies

(1)   Have you ever been in a field at night and sometimes seen little flying specks of light around? Well, if you were to look at one up close you'd realize that these lights are really bugs! These bugs are called fireflies. When you look close-up, you can see that fireflies have soft bodies, compound eyes and a bright, glowing rear end. The firefly's larvae look almost exactly like fully grown fireflies, except that they don't have the compound eyes the adults have.

(2)   Fireflies are among the most familiar insects. They belong to the Family Lampyridae. Lampyrids are able to flash their lights on and off, unlike other luminescent insects which glow continuously. The flashing rhythm is different in various species.

(3)   Like many other beetles, fireflies are brownish or blackish in color. Fireflies are medium-sized insects from 1/4 to 3/4 inches long. The sheath or covering that protects the wings is fairly soft. The protective shield (pronotum) extends forward beyond the body to hide the head from above. Females may be short-winged or wingless. The last 2 or 3 segments of the abdomen have a green, yellow, or orange luminous organ. The light comes from many tiny air tubes (tracheoles). They contain unstable molecules that break down to create light. The light on the firefly's tail does not feel warm to the touch.

(4)   Fireflies (or lightning bugs, as they are called in some parts in the United States) are found everywhere in the world usually in marshes and forests so that there are places that have enough food for the firefly's young. The firefly is so widespread that in some parts of the United States, the firefly is known by both the name firefly and the term "lightning bug". They are also known as "glowing bug".

(5)   Fireflies spend a lot of time clinging to foliage, tree trunks, and branches. Some live in moist places under debris and decaying vegetation on the ground. Others are found beneath bark and decaying vegetation.

(6)   Pyralis Fireflies are found east of the Rocky Mountains. They are usually seen in meadows. The Skintilating Firefly is found from New England to Kansas and Texas. Fireflies in the Pennsylvania Family are found from the Atlantic Coast to Texas and north to Manitoba. They live in meadows and open woods.

(7)   Fireflies are predatory when young, but as adults they usually eat plant pollen and nectar. This mixed diet depends on the type of species of firefly as there are around 2,000 different firefly species. The larvae of the firefly mainly eat the larvae of snails and slugs. They catch their prey usually by spitting digestive fluids (like spit and stomach acid) at their prey using organs near their mouth known as mandibles.

(8)   Adults are not known to feed, but they are sometimes attracted to moth baits. Firefly larvae prey on small animals, insect larvae, snails, and slugs.

(9)   Pennsylvania Fireflies eat soft bodied insects, snails, slugs, and mites. They also eat members of their own species.

(10)   It is not well known how fireflies actually protect themselves.

(11)   Both fireflies and their larva are luminescent. The light may serve as a warning to predators that they do not taste good.

(12)   The firefly's well-known behavior is its bright rear end which is used usually around mating. The process that makes the firefly's rear end glow is known as lighting, which is caused by the firefly's special organs inside itself. Most species of firefly are also nocturnal. Some species of firefly surprisingly do not have the glowing rear end and are diurnal which means that they are active at daytime like humans are. Some of these non-bright species glow when they are under shade though.

(13)   Fireflies have trouble surviving in captivity. In just a few minutes after capture, the regular rhythm of their flashes is lost and the light slowly fades.

9. The author includes a few unknown words like "luminescent" and "diurnal" in the passage. How does the author help the reader figure out the meanings of these words in the passage? (10 POINTS)

_____

_____

_____

_____

_____

_____

_____

_____

10. If a child wanted to catch fireflies and put them in a jar, explain the survival rate of the fireflies and why this is so, using evidence from the passage. (10 POINTS)

_____

_____

_____

_____

_____

_____

_____

11. What is the relationship between the words "firefly" and "lightning bug" based on the way they are described in the passage? (10 POINTS)

_____

_____

_____

_____

_____

_____

_____

Directions: Read the rewritten passage of "After Twenty Years." Then answer questions 12-13.

After Twenty Years

(1)　　The policeman moved up the avenue impressively. The impressiveness was normal and not for show because the people on the street were few. The time was barely 10 o'clock at night, but chilly gusts of wind with a taste of rain in them had caused the streets to be almost empty.

(2)　　Trying doors as he went, the policeman twirlied his club with many movements, turned now and then to look down the street. The officer, with his determined form and slight swagger, made a fine picture of a guardian of the peace. The area was one that kept early hours. Now and then you might see the lights of a cigar store or of an all-night lunch counter, but the majority of the doors belonged to business places that had long since been closed.

(3)　　Then about halfway down a certain block the policeman suddenly slowed his walk. In the doorway of a darkened hardware store a man leaned with an unlit cigar in his mouth. As the policeman walked up to him the man spoke up quickly.

(4)　　"It's all right, officer," he said, reassuringly. "I'm just waiting for a friend. It's an appointment made twenty years ago. Sounds a little funny to you, doesn't it? Well, I'll explain if you'd like to make certain it's all normal. About that long ago there used to be a restaurant where this store stands. It was called 'Big Joe' Brady's restaurant."

(5)　　"Until five years ago," said the policeman. "It was torn down then."

(6)　　The man in the doorway struck a match and lit his cigar. The light showed a pale, square-jawed face with strong eyes, and a little white scar near his right eyebrow. His scarfpin was a large diamond, oddly set.

(7)　　"Twenty years ago to-night," said the man, "I dined here at 'Big Joe' Brady's with Jimmy Wells, my best friend, and the finest man in the world. He and I were raised here in New York just like two brothers together. I was eighteen and Jimmy was twenty. The next morning I was to start for the West to make my fortune. You couldn't have dragged Jimmy out of New York. He thought it was the only place on earth. Well, we agreed that night that we would meet here again exactly twenty years from that date and time no matter what our conditions might be or from what distance we might have to come. We figured that in twenty years each of us ought to have our lives worked out and our fortunes made whatever they were going to be."

(8)　　"It sounds pretty interesting," said the policeman. "Rather a long time between the meeting, though. It seems to me. Haven't you heard from your friend since you left?"

(9)　　"Well, yes, for a time we corresponded," said the other. "But after a year or two we lost track of each other. You see, the West is a pretty big place, and I kept moving around. It is pretty lively. I know Jimmy will meet me here if he's alive, for he always was the truest old chap in the world. He'll never forget. I came a thousand miles to stand in this door tonight, and it's worth it if my old partner turns up."

(10)   The waiting man pulled out a handsome watch. The lids of it set with small diamonds.

(11)   "Three minutes to ten," he announced. "It was exactly ten o'clock when we parted here at the restaurant door."

(12)   "Did pretty well out West, didn't you?" asked the policeman.

(13)   "You bet! I hope Jimmy has done half as well. He was a kind of slowpoke though, good fellow as he was. I've had to compete with some of the sharpest people competing for the same job. A man gets in a groove in New York. It takes the West to bring him out of his shell."

(14)   The policeman twirled his club and took a step or two.

(15)   "I'll be on my way. Hope your friend comes around all right. Going to leave if he doesn't show up on time?"

(16)   "I should say not!" said the other. "I'll give him half an hour at least. If Jimmy is alive on earth, he'll be here by that time. So long, officer."

(17)   "Good night, sir," said the policeman, passing on along and making his rounds, trying doors as he went.

(18)   There was now a fine, cold drizzle falling, and the wind had risen from its uncertain puffs into a steady blow. The few passengers in that quarter hurried miserably and silently along with coat collars turned high and pocketed hands. In the door of the hardware store the man who had come a thousand miles to fill an appointment with the friend of his youth, smoked his cigar and waited.

12. Describe the connection among Jimmy Wells, Bob—the man waiting, and the police officer. (10 POINTS)

_____

_____

_____

_____

_____

_____

13. In what way are the following characters from the story portrayed by both the author's description and the characters' dialogue? In an essay, explain how they are portrayed in the story using what you know about the characters. (22 POINTS)
*Jimmy Wells
*Bob, the main waiting at the store
*the police officer

_____

_____

_____

_____

_____

_____

_____

_____

_____

_____

_____

_____

_____

_____

_____

_____

_____

TEST 2

Total Points: 100

> **Directions**: Read the rewritten passage of "A Newspaper Story." Then answer questions 1-6.

A Newspaper Story

(1)   At 8 a.m., it lay on Giuseppi's newsstand, still damp from the presses. Giuseppi, with the sneaky way who helped himself on the opposite comer leaving his patrons to help themselves.

(2)   This particular newspaper was, according to its custom and design, an educator, a guide, a monitor, a champion and a household counsellor.

(3)   From its many items there might be three editorials selected. One was in simple and pure but colorful language directed to parents and teachers, criticizing corporal punishment for children.

(4)   Another was an accusing and significant warning addressed to a famous labor leader who was on the point of forcing his clients to strike.

(5)   The third editorial was a powerful demand that the police force be supported and helped in everything that they needed to do their jobs.

(6)   Besides these more important editorials was a procedure laid out by the editor in the heart-to-heart column in the specific case of a young man who had complained of the stubbornness of his lady love teaching him how he might win her.

(7)   Again, there was on the beauty page a complete answer to a young lady who wanted to learn how to get bright eyes, rosy cheeks and a beautiful appearance.

(8)   Another item requiring special attention was a brief "personal."

(90   DEAR JACK: -- Forgive me. You were right. Meet me at the corner of Madison and 8th at 8:30 this morning. We leave at noon.

(10)   At 8 o'clock a young man with a tired look and the excited nature in his eye dropped a penny and picked up the top paper as he passed Giuseppi's stand. A sleepless night had left him a late riser. There was an office to be reached by nine, and a shave and a hasty cup of coffee must be done before getting to his office.

(11)   He visited his barber shop and then hurried on his way. He pocketed his paper, had thoughts for his lunch hour. At the next corner the paper fell from his pocket along with his pair of new gloves. Three blocks he walked, missed the gloves and turned back fuming.

(12)   Half an hour later, he reached the corner where lay the gloves and the paper. He strangely ignored those things. Instead, he looked into the brown eyes of a woman.

(13)   "Dear Jack," she said, "I knew you would be here on time."

(14)   "I wonder what she means by that," he was saying to himself, "but it's all right, it's all right."   A big wind puffed out of the west, picked up the paper from the sidewalk, opened it out and sent it flying and whirling down a side street. Up that street a skittish man was driving his vehicle, and the young man who had written to the heart-to-heart editor for the idea that he might win this woman who now waited at the newsstand.

1. What irony is revealed at the end of the story between the narrator, the woman, and the man in the car? (3 POINTS)
    A. It is unusual to see a woman at the newsstand since most men worked during this era.
    B. The narrator is actually mistakenly meeting the woman who was to meet the letter writer from the newspaper.
    C.   The man was driving to the newspaper stand, but he knew he was too late.
    D. The narrator was going to be even later to work than he thought.

2.   For what reason might the other editorials have been included in the background information given at the beginning of the story? (3 POINTS)
    A. To explain that messages were often sent through the newspaper
    B. To provide information that this newspaper included a variety of stories
    C. To show that the city is plagued with problems
    D. To reveal that many people in the city were interested in beauty and personal issues.

3. How does Giuseppi contribute to the plot of the story? (3 POINTS)
    A. He is a minor character who provides the setting of the story.
    B. He is a matchmaker who helps bring husbands and wives together.
    C. He merely only sells newspapers and has not part in the story.
    D. He takes part as the villain in the problems with the man leaving his gloves at his newsstand.

4. What evidence from the passage shows that the narrator is worried about being late for work? (3 POINTS)
    A.   "He pocketed his paper, had thoughts for his lunch hour."
    B.   "Half an hour later, he reached the corner where lay the gloves and the paper."
    C. "He visited his barber shop and then hurried on his way."
    D. "A sleepless night had left him a late riser."

5. How do you know that this newspaper caters to all different kinds of people and their interests? (3 POINTS)
   A. Because it includes a section of education, beauty and news
   B. Because there is a personals column located in the newspaper
   C. Because Guiseppi's newsstand that sells this newspaper is located in the very city of town
   D. Because many different people purchase this newspaper

6. In what way do you know that **skittish** means jumpy, using clues found in the passage? (3 POINTS)
   A. Because the man notices another man standing next to the woman he loves
   B. Because the man was going to talk to the woman who he hoped he could win her heart.
   C. Because he is driving by whirling down a side street
   D. Because he is headed to the newsstand which is known for making people jumpy

Directions: Read the rewritten passage of "Ladybugs." Then answer questions 7-8.

Ladybugs

(1)   Lady beetles belong to the family Coccinellidae and the order Coleoptera. There are about 450 species native to North America. There are over 5000 species worldwide. Lady beetles are small insects between 1/32-inch and 5/8-inch long. They can be either shiny and smooth or hairy. Their elytra (wing covers) are usually brightly colored orange, yellow, or reddish, with small black spots.

(2)   Lady beetles are almost hemispherical in shape, like half of a pea. They have chewing mouthparts. The small head is turned downward and the legs are short. Head, legs, and antennae are black. Larvae (grubs) are warty or spiny and dark colored. Pupae may look like bird droppings.

(3)   Most of the lady beetles east of the Rocky Mountains were introduced from other places. Lady beetles are found on foliage throughout the world. In the fall they sometimes fly into houses looking for places to spend the winter. Huge swarms fly into mountain canyons in the West where they spend the winter under leaves. They return to the valleys in the spring. Lady beetles are the official state insect of Delaware, Massachusetts, New Hampshire, New York, Ohio, and Tennessee.

(4)   Lady beetle species vary in their feeding habits. Relatively few are hunters. Adults and their larvae are best known as aphid eaters, but they also feed on mealy bugs, scales, spider mites, and other soft-bodied insects. They eat eggs of the Colorado Potato Beetle and European Corn Borer.

(5)   A few species feed on plant and pollen mildews, fungus and leaves. Leaf-eaters eat melons, potatoes, and beans in much of the world except South America and Australia. Larvae of most species feed on aphids, scales and mites. Larvae feed continuously while molting. When the final larval stage is reached feeding stops and the search for a place to pupate begins.

(6)   Lady beetles have several insect enemies, such as assassin bugs and stink bugs. Spiders and toads sometimes eat them. Their best defense is flight, but they sometimes fall to the ground and "play dead." They have bright colors and spots to warn of distasteful repellents. They secrete a bad tasting, irritating amber fluid from the leg joints. This defense is called "reflex bleeding." Larvae release repellents from abdominal glands, so birds and other vertebrates usually avoid them. Ladybird beetles have a safety system based on social groups. When hibernating, they cluster together in great numbers, each one releasing a very small amount of repellent. As a group they make a strong vapor to warn off predators that might not detect the scent from a single beetle.

(7)   Lady beetles are generally considered useful insects, feeding on garden and agricultural pests. Commercial operators harvest millions of Convergent Lady Beetles to sell to gardeners for "natural" pest control. There is no evidence that this method is effective in many types of gardens. Multicolored Asian Lady Beetles were introduced to North America and now threaten native lady beetle populations. They bite people and damage grapes and other fruit. If crushed with grapes, their defensive chemicals spoil wine production. Lady beetles are often helpful to people. During the spring and summer, larvae and adults eat large numbers of plant damaging pests, reducing the need

for pesticides. They have nearly eliminated the harmful pecan aphid and helped control pests that infest fruit trees and damage ornamental plants. Seven-spotted Lady Beetles were introduced from Europe to the United States as a method of biological control. By the early 1980s, they were the dominant species in the northeast and have now replaced the Nine-spotted native species.

7. What risks did Lady Beetles face in nature, and how did they protect themselves from these risks? (10 POINTS)

_____

_____

_____

_____

_____

_____

_____

8. Describe the ways in which the Lady Beetles eat and the reasons for these feedings. Cite 3 pieces of evidence from the passage to support your response. (10 POINTS)

_____

_____

_____

_____

_____

_____

_____

Directions: Read the rewritten passage of "Jupiter." Then answer questions 9-11.

Jupiter

(1)   Jupiter is by far the largest planet in our solar system. It is two and a half times larger than all of the other planets put together. It is the fifth planet from the sun and one of the brightest planets as seen from Earth. Jupiter, along with Saturn, Uranus and Neptune. It is sometimes called a "gas giant" because most of these planets are made up of liquid and gas.

(2)   Jupiter is 142,984 km or about 11 Earths in diameter at the equator. That makes it about one tenth as big in diameter as the sun! You could fit about 1,400 Earths into the volume of Jupiter. It is 133,709 km or 10 Earths in diameter from pole to pole. Jupiter's rapid rotation (it spins around in under ten hours compared with 24 hours for Earth) makes it bulge out at the equator.

(3)   Jupiter's magnetic field is the largest single planetary thing in the solar system. It is 26 million kilometers across, making it about 20 times bigger than the sun. It has a tail that extends past Saturn's orbit. If it could be seen from Earth, it would appear to be five times the size of the full moon. The surface we see is not solid. This enormous planet has a relatively small solid and rocky core. Liquids and gases surround this core and blend with the atmosphere.

(4)   Jupiter is a cloudy, windy and stormy planet. It is always covered by a layer of clouds, and wind speeds of 600 km/h are not uncommon. The storms are visible as swirls, bands and spots. A particularly violent storm about three times Earth's diameter is known as the Great Red Spot. This storm has been in existence since at least 1831, and maybe since 1665. If the storm has existed since 1665, that would make it more than 300 years old!

(5)   The layer of clouds is divided into several bands. The lighter colored bands are called zones and the darker bands are called belts. The colors are caused by small changes in the temperature and chemistry. Each band rotates in the opposite direction from its neighbors. Along the edges where the bands meet, these winds collide and create swirling patterns.

(6)   The stormy atmosphere of Jupiter has flashes of lightning just like on Earth. However, while Earth's lightning strikes may be hotter than 50,000ºC, Jupiter's lightning strikes may go over 5,000,000ºC, which is a hundred times more than Earth lightning, and is more than the temperature of the sun's corona. The lightning is made by water near the tops of the clouds. Due to its magnetic field trapping particles from the sun, Jupiter is surrounded by very powerful radiation belts which would kill anyone who entered them.

Jupiter Facts:
● Jupiter's moon Europa is thought to have a giant ocean below its surface.
● Jupiter's moon Ganymede is the largest moon in the solar system.
● Jupiter is the third brightest object in the night sky, second being Venus and first being the Earth's moon.
● Jupiter has more than twice the mass of all the other planets in the solar system combined.
● Jupiter is considered an almost-star. The smallest red dwarf star was only 30% bigger than Jupiter.

• Jupiter's red spot and the Earth are close to the same size. That means that there is a storm going on in Jupiter that is as big as the Earth!

9. What connections or correlations does Jupiter have with Earth? Cite 3 pieces of evidence from the passage to support your response. (10 POINTS)

_____

_____

_____

_____

_____

_____

_____

10. Besides being facts about a planet, what else do the facts from the passage have in common about Jupiter? Explain. (10 POINTS)

_____

_____

_____

_____

_____

_____

_____

11. Why is Jupiter considered a dangerous planet? (10 POINTS)

_____

_____

_____

_____

_____

_____

_____

_____

Directions: Read the rewritten passage of "Louisa May Alcott: A Child's Biography."
Then answer questions 12-13.

Louisa May Alcott: A Child's Biography

(1)   As much as seventy years ago, in the city of Boston, there lived a small girl who had the naughty habit of running away. On a certain April morning, almost as soon as her mother finished buttoning her dress, Louisa May Alcott slipped out of the house and up the street as fast as her feet could carry her.

(2)   Louisa crept through a narrow alley and crossed several streets. It was a beautiful day, and she did not care so very much just where she went so long as she was having an adventure all by herself. Suddenly, she came upon some children who said they were going to a nice, tall ash heap to play. They asked her to join them.

(3)   Louisa thought they were fine playmates. When she grew hungry, they shared some cold potatoes and bread crusts with her. She would not have thought this much of a lunch in her mother's dining-room, but for an outdoor picnic it did very well.

(4)   When she tired of the ash heap, she waved the children good-by, thanked them for their kindness, and hop-skipped to the Common, where she must have wandered about for hours because all of a sudden it began to grow dark. Then she wanted to get home. She wanted her doll, her kitty, and her mother! It frightened her when she could not find any street that looked familiar. She was hungry and tired, too. She threw herself down on some doorsteps to rest and to watch the lamplighter, for you must remember this was long before there was any gas or electricity in Boston. At this moment a big dog came along. He kissed her face and hands and then sat down beside her with a sober look in his eyes, as if he were thinking, "I guess, Little Girl, you need someone to take care of you!"

(5)   Poor tired Louisa leaned against his neck and was fast asleep in no time. The dog kept very still. He did not want to wake her.

(6)   Pretty soon the town crier who made public announcements in the street went by. He was ringing a bell and reading in a loud voice, from a paper in his hand, the description of a lost child. You see, Louisa's father and mother had missed her early in the forenoon and had looked for her in every place they could think of. Each hour they grew more worried, and at dusk they decided to hire this man to search the city.

(7)   When the runaway woke up and heard what the man was shouting, "Lost! Lost! A little girl, six years old, in a pink frock, white hat, and new, green shoes"

(8)   She called out in the darkness, "Why, that's me!"

(9)   The town crier took Louisa by the hand and led her home, where you may be sure she was welcomed with joy.

(9)   Mr. and Mrs. Alcott, from first to last, had had a good many frights about this runaway Louisa. Once when she was only two years old, they were traveling with her on a steamboat, and she darted away in some moment when no one was noticing her and crawled into the engine room to watch the machinery. Of course, her clothes were all grease and dirt, and she might have been caught in the machinery and hurt.

(10)   You won't be surprised to know that the next day after this last event Louisa's parents made sure that she did not leave the house. Indeed, to be entirely certain of her whereabouts, they tied her to the leg of a big sofa for a whole day!

(11)   Except for this one fault, Louisa was a good child, so she felt much ashamed that she had caused her mother, whom she loved dearly, so much worry. As she sat there, tied to the sofa, she made up her mind that she would never frighten her again. No, she would cure herself of the running-away habit!

12. What events and descriptions lead you to realize that this story takes place in the 1800s? Explain how these events or descriptions helped you realize this. Cite 3 pieces of evidence from the passage to support your explanation. (10 POINTS)

_____

_____

_____

_____

_____

_____

_____

_____

13. How did Louisa and her parents learn their lesson about Louisa running away? In what way did they both stop Louisa from doing that? (22 POINTS)
Be sure to include:
*why Louisa ran away
*when Louisa learned her lesson about running away
*another time when Louisa ran away from her parents
*how her parents changed her from wanting to run away

_____

_____

_____

_____

_____

_____

_____

_____

_____

_____

_____

_____

_____

_____

_____

_____

_____

Total Points: 100

> **Directions**: Read the rewritten passage of "A Lickpenny Lover." Then answer questions 1-6.

A Lickpenny Lover

(1)   There, were 3,000 girls in the biggest store. Masie was one of them. She was eighteen and a saleslady in the gentleman's gloves department. Here she became knowledgeable in two kinds of human beings - the kind of gentlemen who buy their gloves in department stores and the kind of women who buy gloves for their unlucky gentlemen. Besides this, Masie had learned other information. She had listened to what the 2,999 other girls knew and had stored it in her secretive brain. Perhaps nature allowed her to be this clever along with her beauty.

(2)   For Masie was beautiful. She was a deep-tinted blonde, with the calm poise of a lady who cooks butter cakes in a window. She stood behind her counter in the biggest store.

(3)   When the manager was not looking Masie chewed tutti frutti gum. When he was looking, she gazed up as if at the clouds and smiled wistfully.

(4)   That is the shopgirl smile. This smile belonged to Masie's recreation hours and not to the store. The manager was like the investigator or detective of the stores. When he comes nosing around, it is goo-goo eyes or "git" when he looks toward a pretty girl. Of course, not all managers are like this. Only a few days ago the newspapers printed news of one over eighty years of age.

(5)   One day Irving Carter, painter, millionaire, traveler, poet, automobilist, happened to enter the biggest store. It is due to him to add that his visit was not voluntary. His family took him by the collar and dragged him inside while his mother looked among the bronze and terra-cotta statue.

(6)   Carter strolled across to the glove counter in order to waste a few minutes. His need for gloves was genuine though; he had forgotten to bring a pair with him. His action hardly calls for an apology.

(7)   As he neared the counter, he suddenly became aware of Masie's beauty.

(8)   Three or four boys were leaning over the counters while giggling girls stood over the side. Carter would have left, but he had gone too far. Masie already had confronted him from behind her counter with a questioning look in her eyes as coldly, beautifully, warmly blue as the beam of summer sunshine on an iceberg drifting in Southern seas.

1. How is Masie compared to the "lady who cooks butter cakes in a window"? (3 POINTS)
   A. Due to her cool and composed nature
   B. Because Masie likes to bake butter cakes
   C. Because they both work in a window of a department store
   D. Due to Masie's way of interacting with the other girls in the store

2. How is does the manager of the store act when he sees a pretty girl? (3 POINTS)
   A. Distracted
   B. Professional
   C. Unintelligent
   D. Attention seeking

3. For what reason is the store called the "Biggest Store"? (3 POINTS)
   A. Because the store employed a lot of girls
   B. To emphasize the size of the store
   C. To make Masie stand out in a prominent store
   D. To reveal that Masie could become the manager some day

4. The end of the story states "a questioning look in her eyes as coldly, beautifully, warmly blue as the beam of summer sunshine on an iceberg drifting in Southern seas." How does this describe how Masie and Carter look at each other? (3 POINTS)
   A. They both were unconcerned with each other.
   B. She looked at him warmly, but he did not care.
   C. They both looked lovingly at each other.
   D. He looked at her warmly, but she was ice cold.

5. How do the other 2,999 girls in the store react to the male customers, compared to how Masie acts? (3 POINTS)
   A.   Masie acts silly and immature whereas the others act respectful.
   B.   The other girls are acting silly, but Masie acts calm.
   C. Masie acts hyper, but the girls are normal.
   D. The girls act hyper and Masie acts normal.

6. Why did Irving Carter really go into the store? (3 POINTS)
   A.   To go see Masie
   B.   Because his mother wanted to buy a bronze statue.
   C. Because he needed to buy some gloves
   D. Because his mother wanted him to see Masie

> **Directions**: Read the rewritten passage of "Cheetahs." Then answer questions 7-8.

Cheetahs

(1)   Cheetahs are built for speed with a whiplike spine, long legs, and a long tail that acts as a rudder for sudden turns. They are the world's fastest land animal. The cheetah can chase its prey for 274 meters (almost a sixth of a mile) at the speed of 114 kilometers (almost 71 miles per hour) per hour. Both the male and the female of the species are referred to as "cheetahs," unlike in the case of many other animals. Cheetahs can generally live up to 7 years.

(2)   Today, most cheetahs are found in sub-Saharan Africa though a few are still seen in Iran. In the past, they used to be found throughout northern India and Iran. They prefer to live in semi-deserts, savannah, prairies, and thick brush. As they rely upon speed to hunt, they avoid dense forests. Conservation efforts are required in order to avoid the cheetah becoming an entry on the endangered species list. In India, the forests in which many cheetahs live are not secured, and they can leave the forests and travel into cities or villages. In the last 2-3 years, cheetahs have been found in these urban areas.

(3)   Cheetahs are rather dog-like medium-sized spotted cats with long legs and slender but muscular bodies. They have a white belly and a dark stripe that looks like a tear on both sides of their faces. In contrast to leopards, which have palmette shaped spots, cheetahs have round dark spots on their fur. Adult cheetahs weigh from 90 to 140 pounds (40-65 kg) and are around 4 to 5 feet (112-135 cm) in length. Cheetahs are built to do what they do--run! Their long tail provides them with balance. They have a big chest, a narrow waist, and powerful muscles in their hind legs. They have small heads and muzzles, large nostrils for increased oxygen intake, and small round ears. All of this makes the cheetah very sleek and aerodynamic when it runs.

(4)   Cheetahs mostly eat mammals like gazelles, impala, gnu calves, and hares, which are all about the same size as or smaller than an adult cheetah.

(5)   Cheetahs stalk their prey until they are within about thirty meters and then give chase. The chase is usually over in less than a minute, and if the cheetah doesn't catch its prey quickly, it will often give up rather than waste energy. This is because cheetahs use a lot of energy when chasing prey at such high speed. They are very fast runners due to the build of their legs and about half of the chases are successful.

(6)   Cheetahs must eat their catch quickly or risk losing their food to other stronger predators. They will not usually fight with a larger animal over food as risking an injury would mean certain starvation. Cheetahs are well-adapted to living in arid environments. In the Kalahari Desert, they have been estimated to travel an average of 82 km between drinks of water. They have been seen getting their water from the blood or urine of their prey or by eating melons.

7. Using the information in the passage, what would an animal have to do in order to survive being chased by a cheetah? Explain why the animal would have to do this. (10 POINTS)

_____

_____

_____

_____

_____

_____

_____

8. As it is used in the following sentence from paragraph 3, what does the word "aerodynamic" refer to? Describe how that affects the cheetah's ability to catch its prey. **All of this makes the cheetah very sleek and aerodynamic when it runs.** (10 POINTS)

_____

_____

_____

_____

_____

_____

_____

> **Directions**: Read the rewritten passage of "Russia." Then answer questions 9-11.

Russia

(1)   Russia is the largest country in the world in area. Most of the country is located in Asia, but the major centers of population are in Europe. In Europe it shares borders with Finland, Estonia, Latvia, Belarus, Lithuania, Poland, Ukraine, Kazakhstan, Georgia, Norway and Azerbaijan. The Che ancestors of modern Russians were from the eastern Slavic tribes. In year 882 they created the state called Rus. The capital city was Kiev (now in Ukraine), where the rulers from Rurikids dynasty resided. In the 10th century, they accepted Orthodox Christianity from the Byzantine Empire.

(2)   In the 13th century all Russian territory was invaded by the Mongols (also called Tatars), who ruled the land for the next three centuries. During this period, known as Tatar yoke, Moscow gradually came to power. Grand Dukes of Moscow united surrounding lands and in the 15th century finally defeated the Tatars.

(3)   Over the centuries of its existence, the geography and climate of Russia have directed the expansion of its borders as the Russian people seek "warm water ports" in which to be competitive with the rest of the world. This can be illustrated by their expansion down the coast of the Baltic Sea to the eastern edge of the continent and their involvement in Afghanistan in the 1980s.

(4)   In the 16th century, Ivan the Terrible was crowned as the first tsar (emperor) of Russia. During his reign Russia gained large territories along the Volga River. He had no heirs, so after his death a period of unrest begun. After that a new dynasty of Romanovs was started. Under their rule the Russian Empire became a world power.

(5)   During the 17th century, Russia expanded eastward through invasions and exploration. New cities in Siberia (Krasnoyarsk, Yakutsk, Irkutsk) were founded as military garrisons and trading posts. By the mid-17th century there were Russian settlements in Eastern Siberia, on the Chukchi Peninsula along the Amur River and on the Pacific coast. The Bering Strait between Asia and North America was first sighted by a Russian explorer in 1648.

(6)   At the beginning of 18th century Tsar Peter I (Peter the Great) founded a new capital in the North and named it St-Petersburg. Under Catherine II (Catherine the Great), in alliance with Prussia and Austria, Russia eliminated Poland-Lithuania in a series of conflicts gaining large areas of territory in the West. During the Napoleonic wars, Russia was against France. In 1812 Napoleon with his army captured Moscow but was ultimately defeated. The strong winter was very tough for the French army. This defeat marked a huge blow to Napoleon's ambitions of European dominance.

(7)   The currency of Russia is the ruble. Russia is rich in natural resources like oil and gas, and it has the largest forest area in the world. Its lakes contain one-quarter of the world's fresh water. In 1917 the "working masses" of Russia led by Vladimir Lenin revolted against the tsar in the October Revolution. Tsar Nikolai II and all his family were killed. The capital was moved again to Moscow, and

St. Petersburg was renamed as "Leningrad". The factories were nationalized, and the farms were joined into "collective" farmlands called kolkhoz. All of the industry run according to 5-year plans.

> (Definition)
>
> Soviet Union — This was a massive country consisting of Russia, Kazakhstan, Ukraine and many other countries. It was a super power until it ended in 1991.

(8)   During World War II, Nazi Germany invaded the Soviet Union. After the battle of Stalingrad, the Soviets started to drive the Germans out and followed them to Berlin. After the war the USSR occupied Central Europe including Eastern Germany. The Soviet Union engaged into a technological race with the USA. The USSR became a nuclear superpower and launched a first manned space flight with cosmonaut Yuri Gagarin. The planned economy turned to be inefficient, and the people weren't satisfied with the government. The USSR splintered into fifteen independent republics and was officially dissolved in December 1991.

9.   How is the passage structured so that it can be read about how Russia became the Soviet Union? (10 POINTS)

_____

_____

_____

_____

_____

_____

_____

_____

10. In what way did the leaders, Ivan the Terrible and Tsar Peter I, shape the country into what it is today? Cite 3 pieces of evidence from the passage to support your explanation. (10 POINTS)

_____

_____

_____

_____

_____

_____

_____

11. Based on the claim made in the passage that the location of Russia has affected its citizens, what details supports that claim? (10 POINTS)

_____

_____

_____

_____

_____

_____

_____

Directions: Read the rewritten passage of "Fat and Thin." Then answer questions 12-13.

Fat and Thin

(1)   Two friends -- one a fat man and the other a thin man -- met at the Nikolaevsky station. The fat man had just dined in the station and his greasy lips shone like ripe cherries. The thin man had just slipped out of the train and was loaded with suitcases, bundles, and boxes. He smelled of ham and coffee grounds. A thin woman with a long chin, his wife, and a tall schoolboy with one eye screwed up came into view behind his back.

(2)   "Porfiry," cried the fat man on seeing the thin man. "Is it you? My dear fellow! How many summers, how many winters has it been!"

(3)   "Holy saints!" cried the thin man in amazement. "Misha! The friend of my childhood! Where have you been?"

(4)   The friends kissed each other three times and gazed at each other with eyes full of tears. Both were agreeably happy.

(5)   "My dear boy!" began the thin man after the kissing. "This is unexpected! This is a surprise! Come have a good look at me! Just as handsome as I used to be! Just as great a darling and a dandy! Good gracious me! Well, how are you? Made your fortune? Married? I am married as you see. This is my wife Luise. Her maiden name was Vantsenbach. This is my son, Nafanail, a schoolboy in the third class. This is the friend of my childhood, Nafanya. We were boys at school together!"

(6)   Nafanail thought a little and took off his cap.

(7)   "We were boys at school together," the thin man went on. "Do you remember how they used to tease you? You were nicknamed Herostratus because you burned a hole in a schoolbook with a cigarette, and I was nicknamed Ephialtes because I was fond of telling tales. We were children! Don't be shy, Nafanya. Go nearer to him. And this is my wife, her maiden name was Vantsenbach."

(8)   Nafanail thought a little and took refuge behind his father's back.

(9)   "Well, how are you doing my friend?" the fat man asked, looking enthusiastically at his friend. "Are you in the service? What grade have you reached?"

(10)   "I am, dear boy! I have been a collegiate assessor for the last two years, and I have the Stanislav. The salary is poor, but that's no great matter! The wife gives music lessons, and I go in for carving wooden cigarette cases in a private way. Capital cigarette cases! I sell them for a ruble each. If anyone takes ten or more, I give a discount, of course. We get along somehow. I served as a clerk, you know, and now I have been transferred here as a head clerk in the same department. I am going to serve here. And what about you? I bet you are a civil counselor by now? Eh?"

(11)   "No dear boy, go higher than that," said the fat man. "I have risen to privy counselor already. I have two stars."

(12)   The thin man turned pale and rigid all at once, but soon his face twisted in all directions in the broadest smile. It seemed as though sparks were flashing from his face and eyes. He squirmed, he doubled together, crumpled up. His suitcases, bundles and cardboard boxes seemed to shrink and crumple up too. His wife's long chin grew longer still. Nafanail drew himself up to attention and fastened all the buttons of his uniform.

(12)   "Your Excellency, I am delighted! The friend, one may say, of childhood and to have turned into such a great man!"

(13)   "Come, come!" the fat man frowned. "What's this tone for? You and I were friends as boys, and there is no need of this official flattery!"

(14)   "Merciful heavens, your Excellency! What are you saying?" sniggered the thin man, wriggling more than ever. "Your Excellency's gracious attention is refreshing. This, your Excellency, is my son Nafanail, my wife, Luise."

(15)   The fat man was about to make some protest, but the face of the thin man wore an expression of such respect and sappy respectfulness that the privy counselor was sickened. He turned away from the thin man, giving him his hand at parting.

(16)   The thin man pressed three fingers, bowed his whole body and giggled. His wife smiled. Nafanail scraped with his foot and dropped his cap. All three were agreeably overwhelmed.

12. Explain three facts from the passage that suggest that the two men were very happy to
    see each other again. (10 POINTS)

_____

_____

_____

_____

_____

_____

_____

_____

13. Describe in an essay how each of the following characters reacted to the fat man's job as a privy counselor: (22 POINTS)

    *thin man

    *thin man's wife

    *son – Nafanail

_____

_____

_____

_____

_____

_____

_____

_____

_____

_____

_____

_____

_____

_____

_____

_____

Answers

&

Explanations

Worksheet 1: Answers & Explanations

1. C

Explanation: The comparison of the Queen of Sheba and King Solomon seeing Jim's watch and Della's hair is an exaggeration that these important, wealthy people would be envious of Jim's watch and Della's hair. This comparison further describes how beautiful Della's hair is and how expensive Jim's watch is. Option A is incorrect because the queen and king were not actually in the apartment building. Option B is incorrect because even though the watch and hair are being compared to the jewels, they actually do not have the same value. Option D is incorrect because the queen and king lived long ago.

2. A

Explanation: Della saves the money one or two pennies at a time and counts it multiple times; this is done because Della hopes that the next time she counts it, there will be more. Option B is incorrect because Della didn't grow her hair long just to sell it. This was realized after her hair was already long. Option C is incorrect because Della did not work. During this time, usually the man worked outside of the home. Option D is incorrect because Della did not ask the grocer, vegetable man, and butcher for money; instead, she kept extra money by not tipping them.

3. B

Explanation: The word "shabby" refers to something being ragged from being used so much. There are probably tears and worn places on the couch. Option A is incorrect because it is unknown whether or not the couch is old or not; it just does not look good. Option C is incorrect because an average couch would not make her home seem poor or bad. Option D is incorrect because the couch is not unusual, but it is in a home that is considered poor.

4. B

Explanation: While reading the story, one may feel a piteous tone for Della because she is working hard to save money for a Christmas present for her husband, even though she is poor. Option A is incorrect because the description of Della's hair shows that she can make some money for it, due to her hair being valuable. This would be a tone of hope instead of feeling sorry for her. Option C is incorrect because this amount of money shows how much she has to spend, and that amount is only pennies, which does not necessarily reveal sorrow toward Della. Option D is incorrect because women during this time usually worked in the home, so Della is doing what common housewives did during that time.

5. A

Explanation: When the amount of money is revealed and emphasized at the beginning of the story, it shows that Della has just a little bit of money, but she wants to buy her husband a Christmas present. Option B is incorrect because knowing the exact amount of money is given to show that Della doesn't have enough money to buy her husband a Christmas present--not to tell the reader merely how much money she has. Option C is incorrect because Della did pay for all of her items from the grocer, vegetable man, and butcher, but she did not tip them. She kept that little amount of money. Option D is incorrect because Della's emotion is more of sadness and not anger.

6. A

Explanation: The evidence that definitely showed Della's condition of her home is seen through the explanation that her apartment looked like a beggar's apartment. Option B is incorrect because it explains what the entranceway looked like and is described as an average entranceway. Option C is incorrect because the amount of money it is unknown if eight dollars is expensive or cheap during the time at which the story takes place. Option D is incorrect because it states that the apartment really didn't look like a beggar's apartment.

7.   Extinction is one of the main ideas that refers to a whole species of an animal dying out and no longer being on this earth. Another main idea is extermination, which is when the species is killed on purpose by hunters. Therefore, extinction and extermination are related because they both end a species' existence on this earth. However, extinction does this unexpectedly through nature. Extermination is expected because people kill these animals on purpose.

8.   The author uses examples to explain how animals can become extinct through natural incidents and human cause, such as hunting. It is inferred that the animals are killed naturally to show that this is going to happen anyway. He states that "Natural extinction is part of life on Earth." Then the author emphasizes how humans purposefully kill animals, so more animals are going to die. He states that "Extermination is an attempt to kill every last individual of a population or species." The author is against this type of killing when he gives statistics about how hunting has gotten out of control. "The Mughal emperor Akbar killed nearly 1000 cheetahs during his lifetime when the number of cheetahs was already declining."

9.   The headings reveal the topic of the paragraphs, but the reader must identify the way the details focus on the main idea within each topic. The topic is simply one or two words, but the main idea contains more information than the topic. For example, in the third paragraph, the topic or heading is "What did they eat?" The details of "melons, plums, and prunes," and "barley," and "pork, poultry, beef" shows that the main idea of this paragraph would be the Fruits, breads and meats that Babylonians eat. The sixth paragraph's main idea is about their belief in polytheism and the underworld because it states that "The Babylonians were polytheists." The second paragraph's main idea is about the Ishtar Gate and ziggurat because the topic states "the Ishtar Gate and Etemenanki ziggurat."

10. The gods were revered in the way that the Babylonians treated them. They built temples for them and provided sacrifices for them. These were requirements for the gods to help the Babylonians. Likewise, Hammurabi had a code so that the citizens would do the same thing. They would follow these rules and do as they were told to avoid punishment from Hammurabi.

11. In the passage, the ziggurat was described as "special pyramid shaped towers" which is a definition of the term ziggurat. Therefore, the author provided a clear definition of the term. However, for the term "underworld," the author does not give a clear definition. Instead, the author provides a description of the underworld. The author describes it as "a dark and dismal place" where "every soul went."

12. In the fourth paragraph, the boy's father is described as a mortgage lender and also as respectable, which implies that he works hard and the people in the town believe what he says. However, he is also described as being "cautious about spending" which explains that the father might be cheap and won't want to pay a ransom for his

kidnapped son. He is also described as being a "strict, upright man," which leads the reader to believe that he won't give up money because he believes he earned it.

13. The kidnapped boy turns out to be a terror to the kidnappers. He kicks Bill, proven from the bruises and scrapes on Bill's body. Plus, it is inferred that the kidnapped boy's father is cheap and may not pay the ransom because he likes his money.

The essay should follow the format below:

• **Introduction**- The introductory paragraph should include an attention-grabbing statement followed by an explanation of how this relates to the theme of the story or the background. The last sentence in this paragraph should include the thesis statement, which completely answers the question and includes the three main ideas that the student is going to use to support this thesis statement.

• **3 Body paragraphs** – Each body paragraph should include a main idea that supports the thesis statement. Evidence from the story should be included, which may include the ideas from the worksheet.

• **Conclusion** – The concluding paragraph should include a restatement of the thesis statement in different wording and a restatement of the three main ideas. The last two sentences should explain the importance of the essay's topic.

An example of an essay is below:

Imagine kidnapping a boy for ransom, and he turns out to be the most spoiled brat ever. It might be difficult to hold onto a kidnapped kid, especially when the father most likely won't pay the ransom. In "The Ransom of Red Chief," the theme centers around that

doing a wrong deed may turn out terrible and this is shown through the actions of the kidnapped boy and how the kidnappers respond.

The theme that is learned by the reader and kidnappers in the story is that doing a wrong deed may turn out to be terrible. In the story, it states at the beginning that "It was, as Bill afterward said it during a moment of stupidity, but we didn't find that out till later." The narrator is referring to the kidnapping and how stupid this idea was. This proves that their idea of kidnapping turns out to be a terrible thing.

The reason that the kidnapping was a terrible thing to do is because the boy is a spoiled, rotten kid. In the story, it states that he was "throwing rocks at a kitten on the opposite fence" when the kidnappers found him. Even before being kidnapped, the author sets the scene that this boy is bad. His behavior begins with him hurting an innocent little kitten. The boy already proves to be a living terror.

The descriptions of the kidnapper's actions also support the theme. In the story, it is stated that "Bill was treating the scratches and bruises on his face and body." Bill is hurt after kidnapping the boy. The bruises are shown on his body. These bruises were not from minor things, but from being hurt by the kidnapped boy.

To conclude, the kidnapping turned out to be a bad idea for the kidnappers. The boy they kidnapped was a spoiled brat who ends up hurting the kidnappers. Even though people usually don't feel sorry for kidnappers, they might in this case.

Worksheet 2: Answers & Explanations

1.   C

Explanation: Even though the men are around the camp, they do not approve of this new baby coming into the camp. Most of the men did not care that she was suffering. Option A is not the correct answer because most of the men are not sympathetic because they are angry about a baby coming into the camp. Option B is not the answer because the men do not understand that the baby should be in the camp; rather, they are annoyed by it. Option D is not the correct answer because there is no confusion since they know what is going on.

2.   C

Explanation: Since the woman is described as coarse and feared, she would have been tough enough to be part of this gold-mining camp. Option A is incorrect because having a familiar name does mean that you are tough. Option B is incorrect because the men disapproved of the baby, but it does not infer that the woman was tough. Option D is incorrect because frequently repeating her name in the camp does not mean that she was tough. It might mean people knew her name.

3.   A

Explanation: When the loud noise is described in the first paragraph, the noise was different from the noise that was usually heard in the camp. Option B is incorrect because the noise does not mean that everyone is happy, but they are instead upset that the woman is giving birth. Only the noise is described as being different. Option C is incorrect because a contrast is described instead of merely explaining the scenery to describe the background of the setting. Option D is incorrect because the men are not characterized as angry but more annoyed by a baby being brought into the camp.

4.   D

Explanation: Several examples are given about how the appearances of the men do not necessarily relate to other aspects about them. Option A is incorrect because when the author specifically describes ironic,physical abilities about these men, it is not to just explain who these characters are in the story. Instead, it shows how it is not important to have a physical disability. Option B is incorrect because violence is not inferred in this story. Option C is incorrect because the descriptions of the physical disabilities of the men are not revealed due to the dangers involved in the camp, but because he wanted to show that they were not important to being great at something.

5.   C

Explanation: Stumpy is described as the head of two families, as a mother and father, which is why he was also considered to be the surgeon and midwife. Option A is incorrect because it can't be inferred that he came to the camp first. Option B is incorrect because his wealth is not detailed. Option D is incorrect because Stumpy is not described as tough but someone who is experienced in being both a mother and a father.

6.   C

Explanation: Even though the men are not happy about the baby being brought into the camp, the sounds of the baby are heard; that sound is usually not heard in a gold-prospecting camp. Option A is incorrect because the noise is not talking, but the baby's crying. Option B is incorrect because fighting is not going on in the camp at the time the baby is being born. Option D is incorrect because the sound is loud and not soothing.

7.   An asteroid is very convincing as the main reason for why dinosaurs went extinct. Paragraph six states that scientists have found "one type of rare metal called iridium." They believe that "Because iridium is so rare on earth, it must have come from somewhere else like an asteroid." Due to this newly found iridium in the ground, it has led me to believe that the dinosaurs died from an asteroid. A crater was found in Mexico that could have been created by an asteroid, which may prove that asteroids have crashed into the earth at one time. It states that "An asteroid impact could have made such a crater."

8. In the three paragraphs, there is a cause and effect relationship showing in the way dinosaurs may have died. First, it explains that a large asteroid hit the Earth. The asteroid didn't kill the dinosaurs, but it caused something else to happen. All of the dust in the air blocked the sun. Since there was not sun shining down on the plants, the plants died. The dinosaurs who ate plants didn't have any plants to eat, so this resulted in those dinosaurs dying first. Since they died, the meat-eating dinosaurs didn't have any meat to eat, so they died.

9. The author explains difficult words like archeology and petroglyphs by providing definitions of these words in the passage. They are either provided with quotation marks surrounding the definitions as in prehistory being described as "before recorded history." Archeology is described using a dash and then the definition as "archeology – the art of finding and interpreting things that are buried in the ground. Petroglyphs is defined by providing the definition in the same sentence. The passage states that petroglyphs are "stones, giant rock ledges and caves were scraped, chiseled, and even painted with drawings called petroglyphs."

10. History is described as the period of time when written records were kept. Prehistory is described as the time before history or the time written records were kept. Therefore, prehistory can only be discovered through the cave paintings. These are not considered to be written records. Also, artifacts have been unearthed to be studied to learn about this group of people. History has certain records and documents we can examine today. Just like prehistory, history also has artifacts.

11. The main idea of the passage is that there were certain things that historians have used to learn about the history of a civilization or during prehistory. These include cave paintings and artifacts. Cave paintings were displayed on the walls, and they showed pictures of the people doing this. The historians must deduce or infer why these people painted these paintings on the caves. They have come up with many theories. Both prehistory and history have figured out ways in which people lived long ago through artifacts. Some artifacts were explained as well as documents to show what laws and culture the people had.

12. The narrator of the story portrays Nicholas as spoiled and having a nasty attitude. This is evidenced when he puts a frog in his breakfast. Then he put the frog in the bowl so that the "the older and wiser people had been proved to be profoundly about the frog in his bowl." This shows that he intentionally put the frog in the bowl as both a joke and to prove the adults wrong. When he is not allowed to go on the trip, "no tears fell from Nicholas's face" so he is not upset that he didn't get to go. When his cousin gets hurt, her isn't

worried or sad. He says "How she did cry."

13. Nicholas decides to go into the gooseberry garden in order to trick the aunt. The aunt spends her time making sure Nicholas doesn't go into the garden. The cousins don't seem to be having fun while they are on their way to Jagborough sands.

The essay should be written in the format below:

• **Introduction-** The introductory paragraph should include an attention-grabbing statement. Then an explanation of how this relates to the theme of the story or the background. The last sentence in this paragraph should include the thesis statement, which completely answers the question and includes the three main ideas that the student is going to use to support this thesis statement.

• **3 Body paragraphs** – Each body paragraph should include a main idea that supports their thesis statement. Some of the information within the body paragraphs should be evidence from the story which may include the ideas from the worksheet.

• **Conclusion** – The concluding paragraph should include a restatement of the thesis statement in different words and restatement of the three main ideas in different words. Then the last two sentences should explain the importance of the essay's topic.

An example of an essay is below:

Have you ever met someone who just had a mean and nasty attitude? In the story, "The Lumber Room" Nicholas is that type of person who has such a mean spirit. He was not allowed to go on the trip to the Jagborough

sands. This trip actually affects the actions of Nicholas, the aunt and the cousins.

Nicholas is affected by not going on the trip by deciding to try to hide in the gooseberry garden. According to the story, "Nicholas felt perfectly capable of being in trouble and in a gooseberry garden at the same time." Even though he was not allowed to go into the garden, Nicholas was going to do this anyway. He wanted to create mischief for either not getting to go on the trip or because he is naturally mischievous. Nicholas seems to act bad whether he would get to go on the trip or not.

The aunt is affected by the Jagborough sands trip because she must stay at home with Nicholas. Instead of doing activities, "she spent an hour or two in unimportant gardening tasks." It seems that she spends her time watching Nicholas. Not only did she have to stay at home, but she couldn't get anything productive done either. This affected the aunt in two ways which are by Nicholas having to stay home and she had to watch Nicholas so he wouldn't get into trouble.

The cousins are probably the least affected, but they are because one cousin gets injured before leaving. According to the story, "all the crying was done by his cousin, who scraped her knee rather painfully against the step of the carriage as she was climbing in." Since the cousin hurt herself, she was starting her trip off in a bad way. She doesn't seem to be having fun. This cousin didn't seem happy leaving on the trip.

To conclude, the actions changed once the Jagborough trip was established. Nicholas, the aunt and the cousins were all affected by the trip. Hopefully, Nicholas would change his attitude after getting to miss the trip, but probably not.

Worksheet 3: Answers & Explanations

1. A

Explanation: When the mongoose encountered the flood, it went from the bungalow to another family's house. Therefore, the setting changed. Option B is incorrect because Rikki Tikki Tavi did not stay in the same place, especially in the bathroom. Option C is incorrect because the mongoose did move from the bungalow to the family's house, but he did not go back and forth. Option D is incorrect because the mongoose stays in the same country, but he moves to another place.

2. B

Explanation: Rikki Tikki Tavi is described as looking like a cat and having a fluffy tail. Therefore, he is not threatening to anyone. Option A is incorrect because the purpose of describing the animal the way the author did was to show that the mongoose was not harmful. Option C is incorrect because his reactions would most likely not be problematic based on his description. Option D is incorrect because he only portrayed kindness.

3. D

Explanation: The son wanted to have a funeral for the mongoose, but the father thought that they could save the animal if they brought him inside. Option A is incorrect because the son did not want to bring the mongoose inside because he thought the mongoose was dead. The father wanted to help the mongoose by bringing him inside. Option B is incorrect because the father seemed very assured that he could rescue the mongoose, and the son didn't think the mongoose was okay. Option C is incorrect because the father wanted to bring the mongoose inside and the son wanted to have a funeral for the animal.

4. C

Explanation: Unconscious means that the mongoose fell asleep even if it wasn't intentional. Option A is incorrect because being unconscious doesn't have anything to do with how smart something is. Option B is incorrect because the mongoose may have been wet from the flood, but he was asleep due to what happened to him after the flood. Option D is incorrect because the mongoose was believed to be dead, but he was asleep.

5. B

Explanation: The main idea of the story is that the mongoose finds a new home with the father, mother and son after he was washed up on the roadside. Option A is incorrect because this is a minor detail that would be too small to be included in a summary. Option C is incorrect because this detail from the beginning of the story is about the setting and would not need to be a major detail to be included in the story. Option D is incorrect because this minor detail does not include enough information to be included in a summary.

6. B

Explanation: Even though the mongoose is a wild animal, the family trusts him after bringing him inside of the house. Option A is incorrect because trust was not received by the family because the mongoose first lived in a bungalow. Option C is incorrect because the family felt sorry for the mongoose, but that would not lead to respect for the animal. Option D is incorrect because that sentence does not suggest trust and respect just because something was found on the side of the street.

7. The second paragraph is written in a narrative form to explain how the jaguar got its spots. In the narrative, the story uses dialogue and descriptive details. Then the narrative also includes

parts of a plot with the conflict being about the puma rolling in the dust when he was still wet. The fourth paragraph is written as an informative descriptive text. The puma is described with facts about his appearance. It is not written in a narrative form, but simply gives a description of the puma.

8. One of the main ideas of the passage is that pumas are an important animal to the cat family. This is exemplified in the explanations of where they live and what they look like. One key detail is that they live in the western hemisphere of North, Central and South America. Another key detail their appearance: they are light brown in color with other colors on their tail and ears. They are very big and can weigh as much as a human being at one hundred fifty pounds.

9. The relationship between the Earth and the moon is that the "Earth has one moon" according the passage, and the moon orbits the Earth. Another object that orbits the Earth that people may not know about is the Cruithne. People should become familiar with this object because the "sun in a way makes it keep coming closer to Earth." Scientists should always monitor objects from space that may crash into Earth. Also, the relationship between the Earth and the moon comes from a theory which states that the moon broke off of the Earth when "a large body hit the Earth and split off a section of the Earth."

10. The continents are really huge plates that are known to move. At one time, they fit together, but then they broke apart. The ways in which these plates move about may result in different effects. For example, when the plates move together, they can form mountains. If they move together, but

there is space between them, that allows lava to move up through the mountains. Sometimes, when the plates rub against each other, they cause what we know as earthquakes.

11. Water is found on Earth, and it is believed that it is the only planet where water is found. Anything that is alive on Earth takes in water. Therefore, anything that is alive must have access to water in order to survive. However, scientists are not done exploring, and there may be living things that do not require water. So, science has not given up exploring the impact water has on living things and how there may be living things that do not require water.

12. The woman is begging and pleading to Kistunov. She does not accept what Kistunov says to her. She wants Kistunov to accept her pleas and help her, and she doesn't want to take no for an answer. On the other hand, Kistunov is somewhat sympathetic at first to the woman's problem and claim, but he sticks to his suggestion that the woman needs to go to another department because they are a bank. Even still, she continues to beg.

13. The woman appears to be aggressive and timid at the same time. Her timidity is shown through her lack of knowledge about how things work. It seems obvious that the bank would not be a part of the medical department of the army. Also, she doesn't take no for an answer. This proves she has an aggressive side.
The essay should be in the format below:

• **Introduction**- The introductory paragraph should include an attention-grabbing statement, followed by an explanation of how this relates to the theme of the story, or to the background of the story. The last sentence in this paragraph should include the thesis statement, which completely answers the question and includes the three main ideas that the student is going to use to support this thesis statement.

- **3 Body paragraphs** – Each body paragraph should include a main idea that supports their thesis statement. Some of these main ideas and information in the paragraphs should be evidence from the story, which may include the ideas from the worksheet.
- **Conclusion** – The concluding paragraph should include a restatement of the thesis statement in different words and restatement of the three main ideas in different words. The last two sentences should explain the importance of the essay's topic.

An example of an essay is below:

Imagine a person being both timid and aggressive at the same time, when it seems like a person should be one or the other. One might think that there is really no way for one person to be both. In the story "A Defenseless Creature," the woman in the story shows both an aggressive and a timid side to her.

The woman is aggressive especially at the beginning of the story. In the story, "the woman questioning began speaking rapidly" when she was describing her problem. This resulted in her wanting to get her message across to the bank manager. Instead, it may her appear desperate. This is not the only place where the woman displays aggressive behavior.

Another instance in the story where the woman behaves aggressively is when she continues to ask the bank manager to help her. In the story, the manager repeats "but I repeat it has nothing to do with us." He continues to repeat this to the woman because she does not want to accept the answer. She seems aggressive by asking the manager again and again. However, the woman does show a timid side to her.

When the woman seemed like she didn't know who to turn to, she asked her son-in-law, this shows a timid or ignorant side to the woman. In the story, the woman explains that "my son-in-law, Boris Matveyitch, advised me to come to you." This makes the woman seem like she doesn't know how the world operates. She seems disconnected from how things work in society. The woman seems lost but also aggressive.

To conclude, the woman shows aggression and timidity in the story. It is important for people to accept the answer to a problem that someone is giving them.

Worksheet 4: Answers & Explanations

1.   A

Explanation: When someone is stating something in the affirmative, then he or she is saying yes to something or agreeing with someone. Option B is incorrect because it is actually the opposite answer. Option C is incorrect because the person isn't ignoring the question; they are agreeing with the person. Option D is incorrect because the person isn't asking a question back because he or she is saying yes to the question being asked.

2.   C

Explanation: The driver acts as if he doesn't care how the passengers are treated based on the bumpiness of the road. Therefore, when the road or trip is bumpy to the passenger, it supports his lazy and unconcerned attitude. Option A is incorrect because the driver is not necessarily angry, but lazy. Option B is incorrect because the driver doesn't care about the passengers because he ignores them. Option D is incorrect because both the bumpy road and the driver's attitude toward the passengers actually go hand in hand.

3.   C

Explanation: The young girl at first remains calm and quiet so much that the driver forgets she is even back there. However, at the end of the passage, she begins to poke him with her sunshade. Option A is incorrect because she does try to get the driver's attention at the end of the passage. Option B is incorrect because she never speaks to the driver. Option D is incorrect because she pokes him and does not ask him questions.

4.   A

Explanation: When the story describes the little girl in the seat, it describes her as having to prop her feet up to stop herself from sliding due to the bumpy road. Option

B is incorrect because she never discusses it with the driver. Option C is incorrect because the driver doesn't care about the bumpiness of the ride, so he doesn't do anything about the ride. Option D is incorrect because even though the girl is young and small, the ride is uncomfortable because it describes her as being slung around the seat during the ride.

5.   D

Explanation: Even though the ride is bumpy, the girl never mentions it to the driver. As a matter of fact, she is so quiet that the driver forgets she is back there. Option A is incorrect because she is a young girl so she couldn't help the driver with the road conditions. Option B is incorrect because paying the fare in advance was a requirement that her mother did before the girl got into the stage. Option C is incorrect because neither of them speak to each other.

6.   A

The ride is bumpy and seems uncomfortable, but the young girl seems content when she pokes the driver playfully with her sunshade. Option B is incorrect because the young girl would have probably poked the driver with a stick or her finger if she was angry. Option C is incorrect because she doesn't seem bothered since she is a young girl and playfully pokes the driver. Option D is incorrect because she is happy with the ride even thought it is bumpy. She doesn't feel odd or weird.

7.   The hourglass shape is mentioned several times to describe the black widow. It is described on being on the abdomen in the most likely place. The reason for the repeated times the word "hourglass" is mentioned is because this is the key mark on the spider that lets the people know that this spider can be identified as the black widow.

This is really the only way that a black widow could be accurately identified.

8. The topic lends itself to having a dangerous and mystifying tone due to it being about the black widow. However, the author describes the red spots on the body, and he also describes the close locations and the many places where these spiders can be found. Additionally, the author describes how the spider grabs its prey in a surprise move.

9. People today are still living similarly to the way people lived as mound builders. They eat the same types of foods, such as vegetables. Also, people today bury their dead, which was developed and first done by the mound builders. Pumpkins were used and became important symbols of the fall season, similar to how we use them as symbols for fall and holidays like Thanksgiving.

10. Archeologists have had trouble learning about mound builders, the main reason being that there are not any written documents to analyze. This is stated in the passage "Because the people who lived in these societies did not leave any written records." Also, the mound builders did not create an alphabet, which makes it difficult for historians to learn about them. In the passage, it is stated "the mound builders never invented a written language with an alphabet." This makes it difficult to read pictures. Finally, "many of these mounds have disappeared" which makes it hard for archeologists to learn about them from their artifacts and what they left behind.

11. The word inscribed means "written." The way the words or pictures were carved into the surface of the object is the more specific way of describing the meaning of this word. The author suggests the definition of the word by including the pottery and the objects that were inscribed upon. Also, the word "images" are explained as being on the objects through being inscribed.

12. Nuisance means an annoyance. This is shown with both the aunt and nephew. The aunt believes the fact that the nephew won't carry her umbrella is a nuisance, as that was expected of the way men treated women during that time. The nephew finds the way the aunt is acting as a nuisance when she wants him to wear a hat and carrying her umbrella. He feels that having to take off his hat while carrying her umbrella is hard to do.

13. The aunt puts a lot of emphasis on the umbrella and hat, due to what is expected in this society. The nephew doesn't find that it is important. The theme suggests that different generations view behavioral expectations differently.

The essay should be in the format below:

•   **Introduction**- The introductory paragraph should include an attention-grabbing statement, followed by an explanation of how this relates to the theme of the story or the background. The last sentence in this paragraph should include the thesis statement, which completely answers the question and includes the three main ideas that the student is going to use to support this thesis statement.

•   **3 Body paragraphs** – Each body paragraph should include a main idea that supports their thesis statement. Some of the information in the paragraphs should come from evidence from the story, which may include the ideas from the worksheet.

•   **Conclusion** – The concluding paragraph should include a restatement of the thesis statement in different words and restatement of the three main ideas in different words. The last two sentences should explain the importance of the essay's topic.

An example of an essay is below:

The way to carry oneself has changed from when our grandparents were our age. It seems that society has different expectations. In this story, the aunt and nephew place a different importance on the hat and umbrella.

First, the aunt places a strong importance for her nephew to carry her umbrella. In the story, it states "she hoped he might not have reached that stage in his life when carrying her umbrella is looked on as repulsive." She wants people to know that her escort is proper. However, her nephew is young and may not believe it is needed. She strongly wants the nephew to carry her umbrella.

Second, the nephew does not place any value on wearing a hat in public. When asked, he responded, " 'I didn't bring one with me,' he replied." He felt that it was a nuisance to wear a hat because he would be required to tip his hat at passers-by. Then carrying the umbrella would be difficult to do. Therefore, the nephew doesn't think carrying his aunt's umbrella and wearing a hat is important.

Third, there is a difference in the importance of societal standards in public. The aunt sees her nephew as "a boy who was a dreamer." This shows that she thinks he does not want to meet societal norms, which is shown in the theme in this story. The aunt thinks it is more important than anything else. Therefore, this difference seems to rule in this story.

To conclude, the different in the importance of the hat and umbrella is shown through the thoughts of the nephew and aunt. He thinks it is not necessary, but the aunt stresses its importance. Today, things have changed in regards to societal standards when in public.

Worksheet 5: Answers & Explanations

1.   B
Explanation: The hotel or inn is described as one of the best places to stay. It has great artwork on the ceilings and makes the guests feel like they are in the mountains. Option A is incorrect because it doesn't state how long the hotel has been around. Option C is incorrect because the hotel has very few people in it. Option D is incorrect because the hotel does have lots of artwork on the wall, but it is known for its relaxing atmosphere.

2.   A
Explanation: The story could be considered a fantasy since there are phrases and events that could not actually take place. Option B is incorrect because the time of the story is not given. Option C is not correct because the characters did not have supernatural powers; they were just ordinary people and they did not have any extra powers. Option D is incorrect because the story could not have been a fantasy by making the setting Manhattan. The story was set in Manhattan and it could still been a true story.

3.   D
Explanation: This hotel was considered to be almost empty, but it was also the best hotel. It describes the hotel as wonderful and all guests loved the hotel. Option A is incorrect because the hotel attracted all types of people. Option B is incorrect because other hotels are not mentioned in this story or at least they are not compared. Option C is incorrect because it is true that very few people knew about the hotel, but it was not due to its location in Manhattan since Manhattan is a large city.

4.   B
Explanation: A list of different people and the things they did for Madame Beaumont is described and one of them is about the bell boys wanting to help her. Option A is incorrect because this statement just describes who she was and that she registered at the hotel. Option C is incorrect because it just state that she looked rich and beautiful, but not that a lot of people liked her. Option D is incorrect because this just described the she stays at the hotel and doesn't go out into the city.

5.   C
Explanation: This artwork is on the ceiling and made people feel like they were there in the summertime and they were in the mountains when they were really in the hotel. Option A is incorrect because there was artwork on the ceiling that looked real. Option B is incorrect because the artist who painted the artwork was not addressed or described in the story. Option D is incorrect because the guests did not paint the artwork on the ceiling, but they did appreciate it.

6.   A
Explanation: This hotel was known for being the best hotel, but it was also known to be the most discreet among those who frequented the hotel. Option B is incorrect because the hotel was actually described as being a great hotel that everyone who went there loved. Option C is incorrect because it is not occupied much but it is unknown whether it is the least occupied in the whole city. Option D is incorrect because there is artwork in the hotel, but it does not state whether it was the most artistic hotel in the world.

7.   Uranus is a planet, but humans can't live on this planet. You can't stand on the surface of Uranus because you would be "going deep into the atmosphere." Also, the surface would be too rocky to live on because it was a "mixture of rock and ice." Finally, it would be difficult where the sun would

shine on the planet for a portion of the time since "one year on Uranus would be 30,708 days or 84 years on Earth."

8. It is difficult to consider that a planet has anything to do with the playwright William Shakespeare. The moons were named after a character in one of Shakespeare's plays or poems. For instance, Miranda is a small moon for Uranus. It was named after Miranda in The Tempest. Also, Ariel, another moon, was named for another character in The Tempest.

9. The passage is organized by each paragraph covering a topic about ants. Each topic is a part of the ant's appearance or way of living. For example, the second paragraph contains information about the "cities" or groups of ants that live together. The third paragraph contains information about what the ant eats. Finally, seventh paragraph describes how these ants communicate.

10. Ants can be both good and bad to humans. Most everyone knows that ants can be pests because they interrupt a picnic or infest a kitchen. Some ants will bite people and others will destroy your plants in your garden. However, they can also be beneficial because they can eat other pests that may destroy your garden.

11. Holometabolism is a type of metamorphosis that ants go through. There are four stages to this process including the egg, larval stage, pupal stage and the adult. The reason that Holometabolism is included in the passage is because the ants go through a specific type of metamorphosis that is part of the main idea about the ants' way of living.

12. The bear was dangerous because it was an older bear who had been fighting for a long time. The story states "The bear was evidently a fighter because the black of his coat had become yellowish with age." Also, the bear acted like it was not worried about fighting this man because "there was confidence in his walk and arrogance in his small, twinkling eye." Also, the bear seems upset when it states that "his blood burning."

13. The little man seems like a wimp because he runs around a lot. The bear seems cocky that he can easily kill this man.

The essay should be in the format below:

•   **Introduction-** The introductory paragraph should include an attention-grabbing statement, followed by an explanation of how this relates to the theme of the story or the background. The last sentence in this paragraph should include the thesis statement which completely answers the question and includes the three main ideas that the student is going to use to support this thesis statement.

•   **3 Body paragraphs** – Each body paragraph should include a main idea that supports their thesis statement. Some of the information in these paragraphs should come from evidence from the story, which may include the ideas from the worksheet.

•   **Conclusion** – The concluding paragraph should include a restatement of the thesis statement in different words and restatement of the three main ideas in different words. Then the last two sentences should explain the importance of the essay's topic.

An example of an essay is below:

If you get attacked by a bear, it is important for you to appear big, which frightens the bear. It may seem scary to do that, but bears can sense fear. In the story, "A Tent in Agony," the bear acts cocky and the man acts wimpy.

The bear acts cocky by knowing his thoughts in the story. In the story, "A Tent in Agony," it states "The bear interpreted this as a challenge." The bear seems that it wants to fight. He makes comments about how easy it will be to injure the man. This cockiness makes the bear think that he will kill the man.

The man acts wimpy because he runs from the bear. In the story, it states "In desperation the little man flew into the tent." It does seem logical that a man would be scared if he was chased by a bear. However, the man seems more wimpy than others. This personality can be seen through the man's actions.

Together, these actions can be seen through the bear's and man's actions. In the story, it states "The little man crouched in a distant corner. The bear advanced, creeping, his blood burning." Both the bear and man are acting according to what is expected. However, they both go to the extreme. Their actions deliberately show the bear's and man's personality.

Even if the bear or man didn't act or have an encounter, they would still have the same personalities. The bear would still be cocky and the man would still be wimpy. Therefore, they should remain and be happy with who they are.

Worksheet 6: Answers & Explanations

1. A
Explanation: The buildings are big and gray, like the mountains. Option B is incorrect because it seems that mountains are made for climbing, whereas buildings are where people work. Option C is incorrect because the buildings are where people work, so they are usually not beautiful but functional. Option D is incorrect because the buildings are not described as coming to a peak.

2. A
Explanation: Fourth Avenue are described as a terrible street, whereas the other streets like Union and some others are described in great detail, but Fourth Avenue is frowned upon. Option B is incorrect because the other streets are described as superior. Option C is incorrect because the other streets are definitely described in much better regards than Fourth Avenue. Option D is incorrect because they are not described similarly; Fourth Avenue is described as a terrible street.

3. B
Explanation: It seems as if Fourth Avenue is described as having antiques that have human qualities, and they are described in a haunting and threatening way. Option A is incorrect because the street is described as having a lot of antiques on them, but it doesn't mention that it is the only street with antiques on them. Option C is incorrect because it seems that where it crosses over another street is the highlight of this avenue. Option D is incorrect because it is not the only thing interesting on the street; it doesn't necessarily describe the antique stores as being interesting.

4. B
Explanation: The street "is never seen again" which means that the street ends at the tunnel. Option A is incorrect because the street doesn't widen especially in a tunnel, but it ends. Option C is incorrect because even though it states that there was a "shriek and a crash," that describes the Fourth Avenue and not cars on that avenue. Option D is incorrect because the street actually turns sharply before going into the tunnel.

5. C
Explanation: The antiques, especially the knights and those that resemble a human being, are turned in the windows of the antique stores to face the street. Option A is incorrect because these antiques are not real people so they can't act as guards. Option B is incorrect because they are not ghosts, but the antiques in the stores. Option D is incorrect because they are antiques and not real people.

6. D
Explanation: The Quigg restaurant is described in a sad way because the author uses depressing words to describe the restaurant on Fourth Avenue. Option A is incorrect because the food is not necessarily described. Option B is incorrect because this restaurant is not an icon in the city; instead, it is considered a terrible restaurant that is located on a terrible street. Option C is incorrect because it is actually the opposite where the restaurant is deemed to be sad.

7. First, it is important to be aware of the tiger because they can pounce and hurt people. Also, it is known that they could be a threat to people if the tiger hasn't eaten in a while and can't find its prey. However, the main thing that a person could do to not get attacked by a tiger is to create a mask and wear it on the back of the head. This way, the tiger will think that it is staring at you. Since tigers attack from the back, they will never be able to find the back of a person's head.

8. The main idea is conveyed by showing the length of a tiger as being "6ft to 9 ft" long. Also the passage describes its teeth and jaws as being "very strong." Third, the tiger is described as being able to hide in the jungle before it attacks. It is stated in the passage that "their stripes act as camouflage."

9. Sweyn Haraldssen was viewed as violent because in the passage he is shown as being involved in many raids. As a matter of fact, he was involved in raids that lasted from 1003 to 1012. Before then, he was involved in a massacre involving the Dutch inhabitants. Besides that, he required several places where he landed to give him some hostages.

10. Hostages were mentioned several times throughout the passage. That is because Sweyn Haraldssen required these hostages when he took over an area. For instance, when he went to Oxford, the townspeople gave him hostages. Also, he was given hostages after the townspeople bowed down to him at Northumbria.

11. "London Bridge is Falling Down" is a very popular song that came from London. Its origins are when Sweyn came to London. He was able to cause the townspeople to destroy the bridge over the River Thames so that Sweyn could not reach the townspeople. The good thing is that Sweyn retreated away from London, mainly due to the destruction of the bridge. This is where the song derives from

12. Irony is when something happens that is not expected. In this case, the private was executed due to misbehavior and slapping his officer. He was executed the next day. However, during roll call,

he answered roll when his name was called. Then the private was executed again.

13. Private Greene's attitude changed from being comfortable with his actions to being scared and then to being proud.

The essay should be in the format below:

• **Introduction**- The introductory paragraph should include an attention-grabbing statement. Then an explanation of how this relates to the theme of the story or the background. The last sentence in this paragraph should include the thesis statement, which completely answers the question and includes the three main ideas that the student is going to use to support this thesis statement.

• **3 Body paragraphs** – Each body paragraph should include a main idea that supports their thesis statement. Some of the information in these paragraphs should be evidence from the story, which may include the ideas from the worksheet.

• **Conclusion** – The concluding paragraph should include a restatement of the thesis statement in different words and restatement of the three main ideas in different words. Then the last two sentences should explain the importance of the essay's topic.

An example of an essay is below:

Can someone die twice? It seems impossible, but there have been stories of people coming back from the dead. In this story, Private Greene is executed, but his attitude changes throughout the story.

At the beginning of the story, Private Greene doesn't think it is a big deal that he hit his officer. In the story, Greene states "that is what you used to do at school." This shows that he did not feel bad about it. He was used to doing things like that. Therefore, Greene's attitude was comfortable.

Right before his execution, Private Greene was scared that he was going to be executed. In the story, it states "there was no reply" from Greene when talking about the execution. His silence seems to be fear. He knew that there was nothing that could be done. He was executed shortly after.

Finally, Greene seems proud when he calls out during roll call. He states "Once more came the name of the dead man." When Greene continues to say here, he seems to say it with pride. He is happy that he is still there. He was executed but came back.

Therefore, the execution of Greene brought about many different attitudes. As the day came closer, Greene's attitude changed. It makes one wonder whether people are really dead after all.

Worksheet 7: Answers & Explanations

1. C

Explanation: The real estate market must have suffered with the flood. The water flooded the homes before they could be sold. Option A is incorrect because the flood didn't necessarily affect his house as it did his business. Option B is incorrect because the former Captain didn't make any money from his real estate business because he couldn't sell any houses due to the flooding. Option D is incorrect because the former Captain quit his job.

2. B

Explanation: Ironically, the former Captain wanted to make more money, but he ended up making nothing because of his lucrative career. Option A is incorrect because he quit the police force—he was not shot. Option C is incorrect because he probably liked being the police officer, but he wanted more money. Option D is incorrect because he wanted to go into real estate for the money.

3. B

Explanation: The man became a homeless person, which is inferred due to how his life was described as not having enough money when he sat down at the lunch counter. Option A is incorrect because he did not become a teacher. Option C is incorrect because you can infer that this man was unemployed because he did not work at all. Option D is incorrect because he was not working at all. Therefore, he was not a laborer.

4. D

Explanation: Young Murray saw the former Captain trying to get fruit from a woman who was selling them on the street because he was hungry. Option A is incorrect because the story never mentioned young Murray's house. Option B is incorrect because young Murray did sit down and speak to the former Captain, but that was after he saw the former Captain begging for fruit. Option C is incorrect because the woman was selling apples—not the former Captain.

5. C

Explanation: Young Murray is described as wearing dingy clothing; therefore, he must be in the same dire situation as the former Captain. Option A is incorrect because it is not known in the passage where young Murray was sleeping. Option B is incorrect because young Murray doesn't walk in an unusual way. Option D is incorrect because no words are exchanged about how young Murray is doing.

6. B

Explanation: The former Captain was kicked out onto the asphalt when he couldn't pay for his lunch at the counter. The woman would not give him any apples even though he had been the former Captain. Option A is incorrect because the others were not sympathetic to the former Captain; they didn't care about him. Option C is incorrect because they certainly didn't act like he was the former Captain of the police department. Option D is incorrect because he was not rich and he was not treated as such.

7. The Oort Cloud contains objects that orbit, but they orbit far away from the sun. The objects that it contain include rock and ice. This is important because these objects could create a problem if they came close to earth. Their distance from the sun is one hundred thousand times further away than the distance from the Earth to the sun.

8. It seems that the Oort cloud was discovered long ago before it even

became known. Jan Oort, a Dutch astronomer, is given credit with the discovery, and it was named after him. However, it did not necessarily begin with him. Instead, it began long ago, and Oort further advanced it.

9. The Romans were a very sophisticated group of people. They constructed buildings that were so strong that they still stand today. They were "huge works of white marble." Also, other buildings were built for entertainment, including "temples, marketplaces, forum and amphitheaters." Finally, they also had a form of plumbing because they had "aqueducts and sewers."

10. The type of house one occupied in ancient Rome depended upon his status. If one was wealthy, he had a better home because it had a courtyard, garden and bigger rooms. However, the middle class had small rooms and a courtyard, but they usually did not have a garden. Those people who were not as rich would live in apartments, but poor families only lived in one or two rooms.

11. Today, people can still see how people lived during the Roman times because there are still ruins to be seen. The buildings were built with marble so they withstood the years. As a matter of fact, the top floors of certain apartment buildings still stand today near Capitolium and Aracoeli.

12. The dog was definitely not helpful to the man. Instead, he probably hindered him somewhat because he would shake and hide. He did nothing to help fight off the snake. Instead, the man had to get a weapon to defend himself and the dog from the rattlesnake.

13. The snake plans to bite by pulling back and jerking forward. The man's plan includes hitting the snake with a stick.

The essay should be in the format below:

- **Introduction**- The introductory paragraph should include an attention-grabbing statement at the beginning, followed by an explanation of how this relates to the theme of the story or the background. The last sentence in this paragraph should include the thesis statement, which completely answers the question and includes the three main ideas that the student is going to use to support this thesis statement.
- **3 Body paragraphs** – Each body paragraph should include a main idea that supports their thesis statement. Some of the information in the paragraphs should be evidence from the story which, may include the ideas from the worksheet.
- **Conclusion** – The concluding paragraph should include a restatement of the thesis statement in different words and restatement of the three main ideas in different words. Then the last two sentences should explain the importance of the essay's topic.

An example of an essay is below:

Rattlesnakes are not always easily seen. They may hide, and their skin can camouflage with their surroundings. In the story, the snake tries to attack the man and his dog by following his own plan. The man also has his own plan to fight the snake.

First, the snake's plan includes striking by throwing its head out to attack. In the story, "instantly the snake's body shot forward in a low, hard spring." This caused the snake to have an advantage by using its spring-like neck to move back and forth. The snake is also used to attacking. Therefore, its plan is helpful for his success.

Second, the man's plan includes using a stick. In the story, the "man jumped and swung his stick." This was the only weapon he had. He only had to watch out for the snake to retaliate. Therefore, the man had a good plan.

The man's plan was better than the snake's plan. This is because the man caused a
"sweeping blow fell upon the snake's head." This would stun the snake. Then the man could continue hitting the snake. Therefore, the plan of the man was better.

To conclude, the man and snake had plans to win this battle. However, the man's plan was better since he had a stick to use. When hiking, it is best to carry a stick to ward off the snakes.

TEST 1: Answers & Explanations

1. B
Explanation: Dr. Chevalier remembered another event that reminded him of the current death. The feelings from both families are similar. Option A is incorrect because he doesn't seem to show sympathy to either family. Option C is incorrect because it is unknown whether the family had an earlier death because the two families were not related. Option D is incorrect because their feelings were similar and not contrasting.

2. A
Explanation: The family members were acting differently, even though they were crying. The doctor would be able to figure this out after encountering so many deceased victims. Option B is incorrect because the manner of her death is only briefly described. Option C is incorrect because the family knew the girl had died and, they crying about her. Option D is incorrect because it wasn't that they were speaking oddly about the deceased, but they were acting differently.

3. A
Explanation: Unfortunately, when the doctor had to invent tender words to the family, that probably means that he did not feel sympathy for them. Option B is incorrect because he didn't feel sympathy or bad for either the person or family. Option C is incorrect because he didn't show signs of helping the family; he simply did his job. Option D is incorrect because he knew what to say by inventing words.

4. C
Explanation: If someone is waiting until something blows over, that means that they are waiting for people to stop thinking about it or talking about it. Option A is incorrect because the town accepted what the doctor did and would not fire him.

Option B is incorrect because the doctor was not fired because the people decided to give him another chance. Option D is incorrect because it is not known whether a crime took place.

5. D
Explanation: When the doctor cared for the remains of someone who was of low standing, it suggests that he cared for people. Option A is incorrect because this statement means that he did not feel sympathy for the family. Option B is incorrect because this statement means that he did his job according to what he was supposed to do. Option C is incorrect because this just states the condition and state of the girl.

6. A
Explanation: The beginning of the story describes the setting by stating that the place where the doctor practiced was loud with screams. Option B is incorrect because the suburbs might be quieter and this setting was loud. Option C is incorrect because he probably is located in the middle of the city due to the loud noises. Option D is incorrect because he practiced on a loud street and not a quiet street.

7. Hammurabi became a part of the Babylonian history due to his strict laws. No other leader had been as strict, so he gained popularity due to his strict way of controlling the citizens. He creates laws that people could read because they had been carved on stone tablets. Also, these were the first set of written laws. They determined whether the person was innocent or guilty, as well as the punishment they would receive. Therefore, due to having such an unusual way of making sure the citizens acted appropriately and they were the first set of laws established for a civilization, he became a key leader in the Babylonian history.

8. First, anything in ancient civilization that has withstood the test of time is going to be included as a prime part of the history of that civilization. The same can be said for the Babylonians. The Ishtar Gate was made of beautiful and sturdy materials, the blue glazed tiles. Plus, the doors and top of the structure was made of cedar. Structures of animals like the bulls, dragons and lions were either carved, painted, or created as statutes in the Ishtar Gates and Processional Way that was inside of the gate.

9. Luminescent is first included in the second paragraph. There are a few words before and after the word that helps the reader know what the words mean. Luminescent is when light is given off which is explained earlier in the sentence when it refers to these fireflies that "flash their lights on and off." Also, after the word in the same sentence, it explains that these insects glow. Diurnal is found in paragraph 12 and the definition is provided after the word. It states that "diurnal which means that they are active at daytime."

10. The fireflies would have a low survival rate because they would most likely die if they were captured. As it states in the passage "Fireflies have trouble surviving in captivity." It is believed that even when one puncture holes in the lid of a jar, that is not enough to keep them alive, and they will still die. That is because there are some fireflies that glow in shade, but others can't be captured and survive. They need to earth and space to move around. It would be seen that these fireflies are struggling as they would not glow as much in the jar.

11. The terms "firefly" and "lightning bug" are used interchangeably, but there is a main difference between the two. This depends on the location of the insects. If a person is in one part of the United States, then the people there might call it "firefly." In another part of the United States, then they might call it "lightning bug." However, there are some areas in the United States where people call them both "firefly" and "lightning bug." Nevertheless, both of these words are for the same insect.

12. Jimmy Wells and Bob are like brothers. Jimmy stayed in the same time whereas Bob left and went West to make money. They both grew up together and were very close when they were in their late teens. They corresponded somewhat during some of the years, but they lost touch after a while. They will be meeting together after a while. The police officer remains quiet, but he is a bystander who walks up to Bob and talks to him to make sure that he is not causing problems at night when there is no one else there.

13. The readers learn about Jimmy Wells in this passage as a guy who stayed in the same town for his whole life. It is learned by Bob when he speaks to the police officer. Bob is a rich man who brags about his riches. He also in a sense hopes that he has made more money and is better off then his friend, Jimmy. The reader learns this by Bob's bragging dialogue to the police officer. The police officer is portrayed as a proud and disciplined police officer who takes pride in his work. This is learned by the author's description of the police officer.

The essay should be in the format below:

- **Introduction**- The introductory paragraph should include an attention-grabbing statement that invites the read to continue reading, followed by an explanation of how this relates to the theme of the story or the background. The last sentence in this paragraph should include the thesis statement which completely answers the question and includes the three main ideas that the student is going to use to support this thesis statement.
- **3 Body paragraphs** – Each body paragraph should include a main idea that supports their thesis statement. Some of the information in the paragraphs should derive from evidence from the story which may include the ideas from the worksheet.
- **Conclusion** – The concluding paragraph should include a restatement of the thesis statement in different words and restatement of the three main ideas in different words. Then the last two sentences should explain the importance of the essay's topic.

An example of an essay is below:

People change after twenty years. It is hard to imagine friends who met in at 20 years old would meet at forty years old. In the story
"After Twenty Years," the characters, Jimmy Wells, Bob and the police officer, have changed and are portrayed differently.

Jimmy Wells is not actually a character in the story; he is only portrayed through Bob's descriptions of him. In the story, "He was a kind of slowpoke though, good fellow as he was." Bob is insinuating that he did better than Jimmy. Jimmy only lived in this town and probably didn't make anything of himself. However, Jimmy isn't in the actual story to explain how he did in his life.

Bob is the man waiting for his friend and he portrays himself as a rich man. In the story, he states "I hope Jimmy has done half as well." He says this to the police officer to

brag about himself. He is also trying to make Jimmy look bad. Bob's demeanor is portrayed through his own words.

The police officer doesn't say a lot to describe his character, but the author describes how he walks as if he knows exactly what he is doing. In the story, the police officer is described as walking with a "slight swagger." This shows that the officer is assured of his position. He almost has a cockiness to his attitude. This is only known through the author's description of him.

To conclude, Jimmy Wells is described by his friend and that is the only way the reader knows about him. Bob and the police officer are known based on the author's input and Bob's dialogue about himself. It was learned that each character is different and through different means.

Test 2: Answers & Explanations

1. B

Explanation: The man who returned for his gloves was mistaken as Jack, the writer of the letter who was to meet the woman at the newsstand. It is ironic that someone different met the woman. Option A is incorrect because women would also go to newsstands even during this era. Option C is incorrect because this is merely an event in the story, but it is not ironic. Including more explanation might make this ironic. Option D is incorrect because this does not show irony. Irony is something that is not expected to happen. The narrator being late is expected.

2. B

Explanation: To better explain how many different people read this newspaper, the passage includes the different sections and editorials that are part of a variety of topics. Option A is incorrect because including these various topics does not reveal that messages are sent through a newspaper. Option C is incorrect because some of the editorials were about problems, but most editorials are. Option D is incorrect because some people were interested in beauty and personal issues, but there were other issues addressed as well.

3. A

Explanation: Guiseppi is a character in the story because he provides the setting where the main conflict will take place. However, he is a minor character because he does not speak or have any main actions. Option B is incorrect because he does not match the people together; he is only selling newspapers. Option C is incorrect because he does play a small role in the story by providing the setting. Option D is incorrect because he is not the antagonist; he is simply a minor character.

4. C

Explanation: The key word is "hurried," which shows that the narrator is worried about getting to work and not being late. Otherwise, he wouldn't have hurried. Option A is incorrect because this evidence just shows what he did and does not make the reader think that the narrator is worried about being late for work. Option B is incorrect because this explains how long it took him to reach the newsstand to retrieve his gloves and paper. It does not show that he is worried. Option D is incorrect because this just shows that he is going to be late—not that he is trying to do something about it.

5. A

Explanation: The editorials that were mentioned described three very different topics. If a newspaper only catered to one issue, there would not be different editorials about a variety of topics. Option B is incorrect because there is no evidence in the passage that there is a personals column. The letter was written to the editor. Option C is incorrect because the location of Guiseppi's newsstand does not affect the number of people that newspaper caters to. Option D is incorrect because it is unknown how many people purchase the newspaper.

6. B

Explanation: The best answer is that while the man is driving, he knows that he is going to see the woman he loves and try to win her heart, which would likely make anyone nervous. Option A is incorrect because at this time, he doesn't necessarily witness any interaction between the woman he loves and this other man. Option C is incorrect because this just lets the reader know that he is driving fast. Option D is incorrect because the newsstand does not make people jumpy since it just sells newspapers.

7. The Lady Beetles are prey to spiders and toads. They have other problems with bugs, such as the stink bug and assassin bug. There are other problems that the Lady Beetle faces, including getting killed by humans and trying to survive natural forces. However, they do have ways to protect themselves, one of them being flying away, which is usually what they do. Other things they can do if they can't fly away is to secrete a mist into the air to keep prey away. Sometimes, like other animals, they will pretend to be dead.

8. Lady Beetles need to eat to survive, just like any other animal. While in the wild, these bugs will feed on plants, vegetables, and fruits in order to live. Some of their food sources include fungus, leaves, potatoes, melons, and beans. In the passage it states "Leaf-eaters eat melons, potatoes, and beans." However, they also are sent to live in captivity. This is because these "Lady beetles are generally considered useful insects." They can help gardeners by eating the bugs from the plants that actually harm the plant. As a matter of fact, "Commercial operators harvest millions of Convergent Lady Beetles to sell to gardeners for "natural" pest control."

9. There are several connections that the author makes when comparing

Jupiter to Earth. The size is one of them, as Jupiter is described as being much bigger than Earth. As a matter of fact, the passage states "You could fit about 1,400 Earths into the volume of Jupiter." Also, Jupiter is so big that its storm is actually bigger than the diameter of Earth. It states that "particularly violent storm about three times Earth's diameter is known as the Great Red Spot." Also, the lightning on Jupiter is hotter than Earth's lightning. That is, "Jupiter's lightning strikes may go over 5,000,000ºC, which is a hundred times more than Earth's lightning."

10. The bulleted Jupiter facts are about Jupiter, but they are also about the extremes and enormity of Jupiter. For instance, each fact emphasizes how big or destructive Jupiter is. For instance, the first fact describes the enormous size of the ocean on Jupiter's moon. The second fact is about the size of another one of Jupiter's moon. The third fact is about how bright Jupiter is compared to other less bright things. The fourth fact is about large mass of Jupiter and the fifth fact is about comparing it to the red dwarf star. Finally, the last fact is about how one spot on Jupiter is as big as Earth.

11. If you lived on Jupiter, even if you had the right equipment to survive, it would still be considered dangerous. A huge storm the size of earth is always taking place on Jupiter. The lightning strikes on Jupiter are over one hundred times hotter than Earth's lightning. Also, the surface of Jupiter is odd, consisting of mostly liquid and

gases, which would make it difficult to survive.

12. In this story, the time is the 1800s. Louisa May Alcott lived during this time, but there are key details that lets the reader know that this story took place in the 1800s. First, the food she had for lunch from her friends sharing it would be odd for today. She said that "when she grew hungry, they shared some cold potatoes and bread crusts with her." This seems like something they would have eaten a long time ago. Second, the job of town crier existed, but it doesn't exist anymore. "The town crier took Louisa by the hand and led her home." Also, people long ago did not have access to cruises or the modern types of transportation we have today. Her mother, father and she "were travelling with her on a steamboat."

13. When Louisa ran away in the first part of the story, she ran away because she "had a naughty habit of running away." She ran away and learned her lesson when it grew dark and "she could not find any street that looked familiar." So, she wanted to go back home and learned her lesson for running away. Earlier in her life when she was two years old, she "darted away in some moment when no one was noticing her and crawled into the engine room." Her parents tried to make her learn her lesson by tying "her to the leg of a big sofa for a whole day."

The essay should be in the format below:

- **Introduction-** The introductory paragraph should include an attention-grabbing statement, followed by an explanation of how this relates to the theme of the story or the background. The last sentence in this paragraph should include the thesis statement which completely answers the question and includes the three main ideas that the student is going to use to support this thesis statement.
- **3 Body paragraphs** – Each body paragraph should include a main idea that supports their thesis statement. Some of the information in these paragraphs should come from evidence from the story, which may include the ideas from the worksheet.
- **Conclusion** – The concluding paragraph should include a restatement of the thesis statement in different words and restatement of the three main ideas in different words. Then the last two sentences should explain the importance of the essay's topic.

An example of an essay is below:

Children today often run away from home, which can be scary for the parents. It is hard to believe that a well-renowned author ran away from home. In the story "Louisa May Alcott: A Child's Biography," Alcott tells about how she ran away, then learned her lesson and how her parents felt when she ran away at age two.

Louisa first ran away when she was a child. In the story it states she "had a naughty habit of running away." Alcott always ran away from her parents because she wanted to get away and play. Her running away from home was frustrating for both her and her parents.

Second, when Alcott ran away, she got scared because the area was unfamiliar to her. In the story, it states "she could not find any street that looked familiar."

Even though the story does not state how old she was, it is inferred that she was relatively young. Any child who is alone at night especially at such a young age will become fearful and want to go home. Alcott became scared and realized her mistake.

Third, there was a time earlier when Alcott was two years old when she ran away while on a steamship to see how the machines worked. In the story, it states "when no one was noticing her and crawled into the engine room to watch the machinery." The parents became worried that she might get injured. They realized their error and punished her strictly when they got home. Even the parents were aware of how much Alcott ran away.

To conclude, Louisa May Alcott was known for running away at such a young age. In the story, there are two accounts of her running away. Eventually she learned her lesson, similar to how many children do today.

Test 3: Answers & Explanations

1. A
Explanation: Both Masie and a lady who cooks butter cakes in window would be cool and composed. The lady would have to be composed if she was making something in a storefront window. Option B is incorrect because nothing is said about whether Masie likes to cook or not. Option C is incorrect because even if this is true, it is not why the author included this comparison. The author wants to show that they can both remain calm. Option D is incorrect because it seems that Masie does not interact with the other girls much due to her calm nature.

2. A
Explanation: It is stated in the passage that the manager makes goo-goo eyes at the pretty girls or tells them to "git." This is said because he is distracted by their beauty, and he does not want to be distracted from his job. Option B is incorrect because he is not being professional by staring at the beautiful girls. Option C is incorrect because the manager may be smart, but he is distracted. Option D is incorrect because he is not trying to seek attention; he is simply distracted by the beauty of some of the girls.

3. C
Explanation: If a store is big, it probably has done very well and has become a prominent store. In this case, Masie works for a prominent store, and she stands out from the other girls. Option A is incorrect because even though the store employs a lot of girls, the narrator calls it the biggest store because he wants to emphasize Masie and her beauty among the other 2,999 girls. Option B is incorrect because the author does not need to emphasize the store just because it is a big store. Not many authors would name their store the "Biggest Store" except if there was another reason. Option D is incorrect because it is unknown whether Masie could become a manager.

4. B
Explanation: The description of Masie's way of looking at Carter and the way it was received was by using the summer and an iceberg. Her look was warm, but his look was cold. Option A is incorrect because one of them was concerned since she looked at him warmly. Option C is incorrect because one of them looked lovingly, but the other did not receive it well. Option D is incorrect because it is the opposite. She looked at him warmly, but he received it coldly.

5. B
Explanation: Masie is known for being calm and cool, but the other girls are giggly when the boys hang around the store. Option A is incorrect because Masie is the cool one and is not acting silly like the other girls. Option C is incorrect because none of them are acting hyper. Option D is incorrect because Masie may be acting normal, but the girls are acting silly.

6. B
Explanation: It seems that Carter is killing time by seeing Masie at the glove counter. His mother made him come to the store so she could buy a bronze statue. Option A is incorrect because he did not come into the store to see Masie; he is there at his mother's request. Option C is incorrect because he needed gloves, but he didn't come in there for that. Option D is incorrect because Carter did not seem to like Masie, and his mother wanted a statue.

7. In order to survive a cheetah capturing an animal, this animal would definitely need to outrun the cheetah. However, the animal would have to be very fast because it is known that the cheetah is the fastest animal on earth. There would need to be obstacles between the animal being chased and the cheetah. Then the cheetah would have to run a further distance. Even though cheetahs are fast runners, they do not run long distances because they get tired from using their energy for running fast.

8. Aerodynamic means to move through the air. The cheetah can run so fast, his motions are descry bed as aerodynamic. Having the ability to be aerodynamic means that this cheetah can move faster towards its prey. If the cheetah can glide through the air during part of the chase, it will find it easier to capture its prey by even coming down on it.

9. The passage is structured in chronological order. This shows that the events that took place in Russia and the Soviet Union are displayed in the order in which they actually took place. The beginning of the passage includes general information about Russia's location. However, then it describes that it begun in 882 and moves into the 13th century and the events that took place in Russia's history. It continues throughout the other centuries about what happened in Russian history before it moves into becoming the Soviet Union.

10. Even though Ivan the Terrible was a troubled leader of Russia as it states in the passage "Ivan the Terrible was crowned as the first tsar (emperor) of Russia," he did contribute to what Russia is today. For example, he invaded and was able to expand Russia by gaining a lot of land. This land is still in Russia today. It states in the passage that he "gained large territories along the Volga River." Tsar Peter I was able to establish a new capital city. Even though it is not the capital of Russia

today, it is still an important city in Russia. The passage includes that he "founded a new capital in the North and named it St-Petersburg."

11. Russia has an interesting location especially in regards to its size. One way that its location affects the people of Russia is that it is in Asia but also Europe. Many of the people live near the European border and area. Also, people probably live near the fresh water that is in Russia. Since Russia contains the largest forest area in the world, many of the people in Russia probably don't live in the forests.

12. The words that the men say to each other show that they are happy to see each other again. However, they also say cheerful expressions to see each other like "Merciful heavens" and "Holy saints." Also, the author includes exclamation marks in order to show great emotion with the characters as if you can feel the emotion that the two men are feeling.

13. The thin man is very impressed and shows it by being very enthusiastic and flatters the man. The thin man's wife acts appropriate that she is impressed, but she doesn't show enthusiasm. The son acts bored and that he could care less.
The essay should be in the format below:

• **Introduction**- The introductory paragraph should include an attention-grabbing statement, followed by an explanation of how this relates to the theme of the story or the background. The last sentence in this paragraph should include the thesis statement which completely answers the question and includes the three main ideas that the student is going to use to support this thesis statement.

- **3 Body paragraphs** – Each body paragraph should include a main idea that supports their thesis statement. Some of the information in these paragraphs should come from evidence from the story, which may include the ideas from the worksheet.
- **Conclusion** – The concluding paragraph should include a restatement of the thesis statement in different words and restatement of the three main ideas in different words. Then the last two sentences should explain the importance of the essay's topic.

An example of an essay is below:

Have you ever found a friend that you haven't seen in years? You might be excited and enthusiastic. In the story "Fat and Thin" the family finds out that the fat man had become a prominent leader, and each character in the family reacts differently.

The thin man is the most excited. He shows his enthusiasm in the story by stating "Your Excellency, I am delighted." He is probably both impressed with the fat man and proud that he has a friend in such high standing. He also is trying to impress upon his son that he has friends in high places. His enthusiasm is shown by his words and emotions.

Second, the thin man's wife reacts normally. In the story, as her husband is all giggly with the fat man's explanation of his job, "his wife smiled." This shows that even though her husband is extremely happy, she shows moderate happiness. This is due to her being impressed, but not overdoing it. The wife's actions and response seem to be the most normal.

Third, the son seems bored with the fat man's explanation of his job. In the story, "Nafanail scraped with his foot and dropped his cap." This shows that he is probably impressed, but he doesn't want to show it.

At his age, he doesn't want to embarrass himself by acting too enthusiastic. He isn't showing his true emotions with his actions.

To conclude, all three people in the family are impressed with the fat man's declaration about his job. However, only the wife calmly exudes her enthusiasm. Sometimes, it is difficult to hold one's enthusiasm in.